C. H. (Charles H.) Simpson

Life in the Mines

Or, Crime avenged

C. H. (Charles H.) Simpson

Life in the Mines
Or, Crime avenged

ISBN/EAN: 9783337177218

Printed in Europe, USA, Canada, Australia, Japan

Cover: Foto ©ninafisch / pixelio.de

More available books at **www.hansebooks.com**

LIFE IN THE MINES;

OR,

CRIME AVENGED.

INCLUDING

THRILLING ADVENTURES AMONG MINERS AND OUTLAWS.

BY

CHARLES SIMPSON,

AUTHOR OF

"Wild Life in the Far West," "A Yankee's Adventures in South Africa," Etc.

COPIOUSLY ILLUSTRATED BY H. S. DeLAY.

CHICAGO:
RHODES & McCLURE PUBLISHING COMPANY.
1898.

Entered according to Act of Congress in the year 1898, by
RHODES & MCCLURE PUBLISHING COMPANY,
In the Office of the Librarian of Congress at Washington.

All Rights Reserved.

CONTENTS

	PAGES.
CHAPTER 1. Introduction—John Beaty Leaves Boston and Settles at Kirwin, Kas.—Two Crop Failures—Starts for Arizona....................	17 21
CHAPTER 2. Suspense—Edith Orphaned—Zack Too Late................................	22 26
CHAPTER 3. Warned—Peril—Called a Halt— Floored—Thanks Endured—A Searching Gaze..	29 34
CHAPTER 4. The Kid Confused—Falsely Accused— Tom's Interrogatories—Approval—Name Withheld—Just Plain Tom.......................	34 42
CHAPTER 5. The Kid's Story—Tom Seeks Light— Jim Madison—A Mystery—Tom Declines Reward —Seeking a Motive........................	45 53
CHAPTER 6. A Brotherhood Formed—Under Tent —One-Eyed Riley Predicts Trouble—A Clew...	53 56
CHAPTER 7. A Morning Stroll—Tom Abhors Cooking—A Venison Breakfast—Tom's Plan........	59 62
CHAPTER 8. One Thing Accomplished—Silence Rather than Falsehood—The Phantom Horseman—Forebodings—Alone—Kidnaped	65 70
CHAPTER 9. A New Pard—The Diminutive Specimen—Efficacy of the Quieter—Faro Bill Advises Caution—Faro Facetious—Riley Shadows Weston—Details Settled—The Swoop.............	70 83

	PAGES.

CHAPTER 10. A Private Prison—Enamored—The 83
Siren Repulsed............................. 85

CHAPTER 11. Confronted—The Lions Bearded— 86
Vow of Vengeance—Faro's Bluff Called........ 91

CHAPTER 12. No Tidings—Aid Secured—Inez Al- 92
varez—Rescue—Tom Learns How It Was Done
—Home Again—A Visit Postponed............ 100

CHAPTER 13. Putting Things to Rights—Dutch John 103
Rattled—A Waiting Policy—Decide to Investigate 106

CHAPTER 14. An Arizona Sunset—Awaiting the 109
Moon—On Schedule Time—Following the Phantom—John Beaty's Skeleton—Jim the Murderer. 115

CHAPTER 15. A Late Breakfast—Comparatively 116
Contented—S.-B. and Hoe-Cake—Planning the
Next Move—Tom's Mountain Home........... 125

CHAPTER 16. At Work—Glistening Quartz—Tom's 125
Judgment Commended—Tenting at Las Animas. 128

CHAPTER 17. Discovery Announced—The Great 131
Dam—The Kid Impatient—The Tell-Tale Blush. 134

CHAPTER 18. Seeking Cover—The Triangle Confers 137
—Land Pirates' Rendezvous—Fugitives Hear the
News—Riley's Listeners Sava—Match in Hand.. 143

CHAPTER 19. To the Mission—An Intercepted Tip 144
—Lola's Fatal Letter—A Late Start—Swimming
—Tom's Unerring Bead—Routed—A Revelation. 156

CONTENTS.

PAGES.

CHAPTER 20. Kid Revives—Doctors Hopeful—Lynched—Long Convalescence—Tom in Love.. 159 165

CHAPTER 21. A Happy Waking—Kid's Boyhood Passed—Tom's Tender Trend—The Old Story—Pleading for Delay—Tom Longs for Home...... 165 171

CHAPTER 22. Farewell to Ruby Gulch—Concern for Tom—"Call Me Edith"—Transformed—Jim Madison Located....................... 172 178

CHAPTER 23. Dutch John in Retreat—Hiding and Plotting—Jim's Bold Plan—A Rogues' Rehearsal—The Trap Sprung—Tom's Close Call......... 181 187

CHAPTER 24. Entrapped—Calmed by Reflection—Whither?—Held at Bay—Captor Entreats—No Let-Up 188 199

CHAPTER 25. Pad Peesness—Dutch John Deserts the Ship—Jim's Forlorn Hope—A Desperate Plunge.................................. 199 203

CHAPTER 26. Courage Is Strength—Help!—Timely Succor 204 211

CHAPTER 27. Love Triumphant—Snugging Up—Tom Obeys the Captain—Kid's Narrative—Grateful Acknowledgment...................... 211 216

CHAPTER 28. On Terra Firma—Made Comfortable—Kid's New Outfit....................... 219 221

CHAPTER 29. Man Hunt Resumed—Run Down—Vain Pleading........................... 222 226

PAGES.

CHAPTER 30. Seeking Passage—Beskirted Again— 229
Pleading with the Captain—Debating—Tom Cuts
the Gordian Knot—Post-Nuptial Cooing............ 236

CHAPTER 31. Ready to Sail—Mr. James and Mr. 236
Brooks—Separation—He Cometh Not—Reward. 242

CHAPTER 32. Jim Madison Puzzled— Behind Stained 242
Glass—In Terror—Tucson Joe Bobs Up - Joe's
Headquarters—Feigns Surprise—The Dungeon.. 254

CHAPTER 33. Held for Ransom—Up a Stump— 254
Higgling—Blackmailer vs. Blackmailer.......... 259

CHAPTER 34. Fred Fears Edith—Desperate Straits 260
—"'Ands Hup!"—Jim Joins Tom.............. 265

CHAPTER 35. Patience Exhausted—Tom's Cordial 266
Greeting—Garroted—Prisoner Becomes Jailer—
Freedom Regained—Sea Nymph Wrecked...... 274

CHAPTER 36. Vain Search—Exit Fred—Still On- 277
ward—Called Back—A Joyful Reunion—Baby
Mine 282

CHAPTER 37. Jim a Cannibal—Sins Recounted— 285
Tom's Seaside Villa—Minus the Serpent—Cliffside's Former Owner......................... 290

CHAPTER 38. Tom's Retrospect—A Mercenary 293
Belle—The Test............................. 295

CHAPTER 39. Benign Providence—An Old Flame 296
Visits Cliffside—Belle's Covert Insinuation—Mischief Scented—News of Madison.............. 303

	PAGES.
CHAPTER 40. Reward Offered—Granny Jones' Gossip—Sweet Angie—Peaceful Cliffside—Planning the Picnic—Off to Santa Barbara Islands.......	304 311
CHAPTER 41. The Picnic—A Remarkable Resemblance—The Veil Too Gauzy—Outing Over—Too Exquisite to Last..........................	312 318
CHAPTER 42. Jim's Thirst for Revenge—A Pliant Tool—Boiling Venom—Treachery—Angie Taken Away...............................	321 325
CHAPTER 43. Cliffside Aroused—Edith Joins the Chase—On the Trail—In a Dead Faint—Edith Inconsolable—Belle Elopes—The Treaty.......	326 335
CHAPTER 44. Edith Plans a Raid—High-Toned Blackmailers—Uxoricide—Edith Forgives Belle —Edith's Vow Fulfilled—The Curtain Falls....	336 343

—:o:—

ILLUSTRATIONS.

BY H. S. DE LAY.

	PAGE.
"Jim Madison Chanced to Meet Her."	16
Edith	18
"By Hoky! Stop ther Train!"	23
Mrs. Beaty Received a Letter Regularly	25
"Don't yer go fer to tell me yer never done it."	28
Glaring upon His Victim	30
"O Sir! I'm not afraid to trust you!"	35
"O God! I Can't Tell."	41
"She was Prostrated by a Severe Illness."	44
"Jim Wrote and Told Us."	46
"He Bade the Kid Rest Easy, and Went Out."	52
"Just Cussing Everybody."	55
"Dropped His Cup of Coffee."	58
Barren Hills and Sandy Plains	60
"The Bed was Empty."	64
"My God! He Has Been Kidnaped!"	67
"It was the Phantom Horseman!"	71
"H—sh! What's All That Racket About?"	74
"Fool That You Are!"	82
Mlle. Laitner	84
"Curse You, Faro Bill!"	87
"I Have a Little Business to Settle."	89
"O Tom!" Cried the Boy	93
"Si, Signor, You Can Trust Me."	96
"Where's Faro Bill?"	102
The Dishes Were All Dirty	104
"The Phantom Horseman."	108
"Directly Over the Heart a Knife Was Sticking."	114

ILLUSTRATIONS.

	PAGE.
They Halted Before the Door."	117
"Tom Went About Starting a Fire."	119
"Tom and His Companion Set Out for Las Animas."	124
Patient, Industrious Toilers	126
Ruby Gulch Dam	130
Down in the Valley	132
"The Man Bent Forward with the Flaming Match."	136
The Mission	139
"On They Urged Their Foaming Steeds."	145
"The Man Fell with a Sickening Thud."	153
"The Doctor Came Every Day."	158
"The Last of One-Eyed Riley."	161
'He Placed the Things Upon the Table."	164
Spring's First Birds and Flowers	166
"She Came Running Down the Walk to Meet Them."	173
In the Garden	175
"What He Saw."	180
"Putting on Her Wraps Quickly."	186
"Stop, Jim Madison!"	189
"She Lay Down Without Undressing "	193
"She Dropped Lightly into the Water."	198
Coasting Along the Shore	200
"Look! Look!" Cried the Old Sea Captain	205
"She Struck Boldly for the Shore."	207
"Hold Her Fast!"	210
Towing the Vessel to Shore.	213
"Just the Fit, I Do Declare!"	218
The Old Sea Captain	220
"He Hurled Him to the Ground!"	223
"A Crowd Gathered About the Wreck."	225
"Edith Emerged from the Dress Maker's Establishment."	228
"If You Had Been Here Yesterday," Said an Old Sailor	231

ILLUSTRATIONS.

	PAGE
"She Found a Carriage Awaiting Her."	237
"Tearing Open the Envelope, She Read."	240
"Hello there—Tucson Joel Whereaway?"	243
"A Good View of the Harbor Could Be Had."	247
"Tom's Jailer Came and Gave Him His Supper."	255
John Mason	258
"Six Masked and Armed Men Entered the Room."	261
"Dogged."	264
"In an Instant Tom was Beside Her."	267
"Tom Sprang Upon Him."	271
"What Is It?" Asked the Girl	276
"Settled Herself for a Long Ride."	279
'Oh! What a Lovely Place!"	284
The Cottage	289
"I Pleaded. I Promised to Toil for Her."	292
"The Girl Who Was to Be My Wife."	294
"Not a Bit Like Her Father."	297
The Grotto	302
"Skimming Like a White-Winged Bird."	305
Granny Jones	308
"The Picnic on Santa Barbara Islands."	313
The Long-Bearded Foreigner	316
"I Must Call at Granny Jones' and See How She Is."	320
"Tom Departed for the City."	324
"O Granny!" Moaned Edith	327
"The Nearest Telegraph Station."	329
"Here Is the Money."	337
"He Drew a Revolver and Fired."	340

"JIM MADISON CHANCED TO MEET HER."
---16---

LIFE IN THE MINES; or, Crime Avenged.

INCLUDING THRILLING ADVENTURES AMONG MINERS AND OUTLAWS.

CHAPTER I.

INTRODUCTION.

From the financial ruins of a great mercantile establishment of Boston John Beaty, the head of the firm, emerged a poor man—to battle for the first time in his life against fortune, which had always looked upon him with a beneficent smile, but now had so suddenly turned her face away.

With nothing but himself and family, and with the whole world before him from which to choose a new home, we find him, after a careful consideration of the possibilities of his surroundings, located upon a small farm near the thriving town of Kirwin, Kansas.

For the first two years he did well. He improved his farm, gathered considerable stock about him, and, comparatively speaking, was quite prosperous and happy.

But, alas for the ambitious hopes of the Kansas farmer! The drought and the hot winds came, when the fields of waving wheat and tasseling corn, bowing down before the withering blast, died.

But the Kansas farmer, though an inveterate grumbler, was not to be baffled by the failure of one crop. It but all the more determined him to try again.

John Beaty was no exception to the general rule. He followed the example of his neighbors by putting in another crop, only to see it, when nearly matured, beaten into the ground by a terrific hail-storm.

There was no alternative. He must mortgage his farm to get money to provide food and clothing for his family during the coming Winter, and then go away to seek employment elsewhere, as many others had done.

"But where will you go, father?" asked the wife, doubtfully.

"Oh, I will go to Arizona," he replied. And that evening, gathering his family about him, he told them of his plans.

"Yes," he said, "I will go to Arizona. They have discovered some new and rich mines there, and there is plenty of work and wages are good; and, perhaps, there may be some thing better for me there."

EDITH.

"O papa!" cried Edith, a handsome girl of fifteen—his only daughter. "We can never stand it for you to go off away out there, and leave us here all alone!"

"It is the best—it is the only—thing that I know of that I can do," he declared. "Beside, there are several others that are going, and—ah! I don't know but that is where the trouble lies, for Jim is your——"

"O papa, don't—please don't! I don't care any thing for him—I don't. You know I don't. I wish that he would go away and never come back. I despise him—so I do!"

"Don't tease the child, father," said the mother, reprovingly. "She isn't old enough to think of such things yet."

"No, no—of course not. Beside, what could I do without my boy—my tomboy?" laughed the father, who loved to call her his boy.

Everything was arranged, and the day of starting at last arrived.

It was a day such as only the Kansan knows when Mr. Beaty, ready for his departure, called his "boy" to him and bade her go fetch the horses from the stubble-field. "The boys will be here soon, all ready to go, and you can drive us to town."

In an incredibly short time the girl, mounted upon her fiery little riding pony, dashed away at a break-neck speed down the road toward the field of stalks, where the horses were feeding.

Edith Beaty, as we have said, was a handsome girl; but today, as she dashed down the road upon her little pony, her long, wavy tresses flying loose, her dark eyes beaming with health and pleasure, most ravishingly beautiful did she appear to the young and handsome Jim Madison, who chanced to meet her just as she was crossing the little bridge at the creek a quarter of a mile below her father's house.

"Stop!" cried the young fellow, seizing the bridle-rein, as she attempted to ride past him without stopping. "O Edie!" he cried, impetuously, "do you intend to send me away without even a parting word? Cruel! Give me a parting kiss, Edie, my love, and tell me that you will remember me when I am gone; that you will wait for my return with the fortune that I shall win in the Far West; that you will share it with me, for I love you, Edie, as no other man can love!"

"Stop!" cried the girl, with crimson cheeks, struggling to check the passionate words that were clamoring for utterance. "Stop! Let me go! You shall not kiss me!" she panted, struggling to free herself from his rude embrace.

"But I will!" he cried, passionately, and, in spite of her frantic struggles, he succeeded in implanting a kiss upon her ripe, red lips.

"Oh, I hate you!" cried the enraged girl, giving her pony a cruel cut with her riding-whip that sent him flying madly down the road opposite where the horses were feeding in the stalk-field, when, without stopping to open the gate which led into the field, she turned her pony's head directly toward the wire-fence and cried: "Over it, Cæsar, you rascal!"

It was no strange thing for her to do, for she would ride the wildest colts upon her father's farm without saddle or bridle; and the neighbors declared that she would never ride through a gate, preferring to jump the fence, even though she found the gate open.

"She's the harum-scarumest critter that I ever did see!" declared Aunt Polly Jones, who lived just across the way.

"A reg'lar wildfire as what no good will come of!"

assented her daughter, who, it may be said, was a bit jealous of the pretty girl.

"I don't care! She's a bully girl—she is; an' she kin lick the best boy in school!" declared Zack Jones, a big, gawky fellow of about Edith's age.

"Yes; an' she licked you, too, yesterday!" snapped Nancy.

"Don't care if she did; I 'd no business a-trying ter kiss 'er," retorted Zack.

"There she goes now! See her go over the fence!" ejaculated Aunt Polly.

"Bully!" shouted Zack. "She's a stunner!"

"She air a moughty fine gal—she air!" attested old man Jones, vehemently, as he ejected a stream of tobacco-juice from his capacious mouth with such precision as to hit old dog Rover square in the eye as he sat blinking in the corner behind the stove.

Up through the field by neighbor Jones', with the horses upon a run, dashed the dauntless Edith.

Arriving at home, the team was soon harnessed and hitched to the wagon; and then, with her father, Jim Madison and two other of the neighbor boys, and their luggage, she set out for Kirwin, where they were to take the train for Denver.

At the depot, she kissed her father an affectionate farewell, shook hands with each of the boys, wished them a pleasant journey, and then returned home.

CHAPTER II.

SUSPENSE FOLLOWS PARTING

All through the Winter and the following Summer Mrs. Beaty and her daughter received a letter regularly each week from the absent husband and father, telling them of his success, which, he said, far exceeded his most sanguine expectations.

After working all Winter in the mines, he set out in the Spring to prospect a little on his own account. In this he had been very successful, for, during the Summer, he and Jim Madison discovered a very rich mine. After working their mine till Autumn, they sold out, and Mr. Beaty started for home.

This was the last that was ever seen or heard of him.

When he did not return, as he had promised them in his last letter, they wrote, but could get no answer. Then, as the other two boys that had gone with him had returned, they wrote to Jim Madison, but for a long time they received no answer from him. But finally he wrote, telling them that Mr. Beaty had dissolved partnership with him, and after selling his property had, as he supposed, returned home.

Detectives were then employed to look up the missing man, but nothing could be learned of his whereabouts or of his fate more than that he had set out for home. Not even a trace of the missing man could be found. Thus passed the long, dreary Winter months.

The terrible disappointment and worry over the un-

"By Hoky! Stop ther Train!"

certain fate of the husband had, at last, prostrated the wife with a severe illness, from which she never recovered. Gradually weaker and weaker she grew until Spring, when she died.

"Poor soul!" said good Aunt Polly Jones. "She has worried herself to death, and no wonder."

MRS. BEATY RECEIVED A LETTER REGULARLY.

"What 'll the gal do, I wonder?" interrogated old man Jones.

"They 've sold out ev'ry hoof, an' even th' furnitoor, fer to git money to carry on th' search with. Don't b'lieve that she's got nary a copper left."

"I axed her to come here and stay with our Nancy, as we was a-comin' home from the buryin'; but, poor child! she 's jest that nigh crazy she don't know which end she 's on," declared Mrs. Jones.

"Land alive!" exclaimed Mrs. Madison. "Did you ever see such carryings on as she did make at the funeral? She just raved, and she vowed that she 'd solve the mystery of her dad's fate, and she 'd avenge her mother's death. I believe that somebody had ought to see after her, or she 'll do some thing awful."

"Bet yer bottom dollar she will do that very thing!"

cried Zack, who had come in just in time to hear the last remark of Mrs. Madison. "She 's a stunner—she air! I jest met her a-goin' down the road, an' when I axed her where she was goin' she said as how she was goin' to Bostin, where her brother or somebody lived, an' she 's goin' to send him out there fer to look up her dad."

"Zack, yer gits on ter ole Kit an' takes arter her," said old man Jones. "She 's not a-goin' ter leave here without no money. Here 's twenty-five dollars as what 's left from sellin' of them hogs yesterday. Take it, an' if she won't come back, give it ter her. It 'll help her a little."

"Bully fer me!" shouted Zack, grasping the money and hastening away to get his horse. In a few moments he was galloping away toward town in pursuit of the girl.

"Whoop!" vociferated the excited Zack, as he dashed up to the depot platform just in time to see the train upon which the girl had taken her departure disappear. "Whoop! By hoky! Stop ther train! Gol darn my hide, she's gone! I'm left!" Then, turning his horse toward home, he returned and told his parents that she had gone for "Bostin, where her brother or somebody lived."

—:o:—

"Don't yer go fer to tell me yer never done it."

CHAPTER III.

THE HUNCHBACK WARNS THE KID.

"Kid! You thar, Kid! Look out! He's gwine ter knife yer!"

These words of warning came from a little, dried-up, humpbacked specimen of the *genus homo* who had just entered the gambling den and dance hall—a low, disreputable dive known as the Casino, in the new mining town of Las Animas, in the northwest part of Arizona— and were directed to a slim, girlish-looking lad, who was engaged in an altercation with a huge, coarse-looking miner, who was apparently upon the point of striking the lad with a knife.

"Poke yer nose in here, will yer? Maybe yer don't know me, yer dried-up son-of-a-whiffet! Whoop! I'm ther rip-roarin' ritudelorium from Bitter Creek—I am! Whoop!"

Thus roared the renegade, and, with a bound which would have done credit to an enraged lion, he sprang toward the unfortunate but well-meaning meddler, and, planting a blow from his ponderous fist full upon the little man's nose, sent him spinning across the room. There, limp and apparently lifeless, he collapsed and lay in a heap till some one, taking pity upon him, dragged him away, groaning and muttering deep vengeance upon the head of his assailant.

Without even one parting glance at his victim, for little did the renegade care whether he was killed or not,

Tucson Joe—the bad man from Bitter Creek, horse thief, murderer, anything that was bad, nothing that was good—turned again upon the lad, and, in a voice hoarse with drunken passion, cried:

"Give 'er up, yer white-livered son of a sneak thief! Give 'er up, or by the Moly Hoses I'll cut yer bloody little heart outen yer!"

"I have n't got it," replied the accused, a lad of some fifteen years of age—slim, almost girlish in form and feature. Almost? No—not almost, but altogether girlish, and with a face that any girl might be proud of, though browned by exposure to sun and wind; large, lustrous, deep-blue eyes, and hair which, though cropped quite short, curled up in golden ringlets all over his round head and drooped down over a broad, low brow as smooth and white as marble. "I have n't got it," he declared.

GLARING UPON HIS VICTIM.

"Yer lie—yer measly little whelp!" shouted the renegade, making a dive for the boy.

"What has he done, Joe? What has the Kid done?" inquired the keeper of the Casino, in a conciliatory tone.

"Done? What 's ther Kid done, did yer say? He 's stole my pocket-book—that 's what he 's done. And if he don't give 'er up I'll have his bloody little liver!"

"I never did it!" cried the lad, defiantly. "I know nothing about it."

"Don't yer go fer to tell me yer never done it, yer—" And he ripped out a string of oaths as long as his brawny arm.

"I never!" cried the boy, and his eyes blazed with indignation.

"O yer imp of——"

But speech failed him. For, so infuriated was he, his voice choked with passion and gave way to a long, fiendish hiss, as, gathering himself together, and with all his fiendish, demoniacal strength and fury, he prepared to spring upon the Kid.

"Hold there!"

These words rang loud and clear down through the crowded saloon. There was something terribly impressive in the ring of that deep-toned voice of command.

Turning like a demon of fury—and he was as near it as mortal man could well be—Tucson Joe faced the presumptuous meddler, fully determined to "lay him out," as he had done the little humpbacked fellow but a moment before.

"Moly Hoses!" he fairly roared, livid with rage and foaming at the mouth like an enraged boar; and with his bleary eyes, blood-shot and bloated from whisky drinking, glaring upon his victim, he prepared to spring upon him.

For a moment the two men, both giants in stature, stood gazing upon each other; and then, like a thunderbolt, they sprang together. For a moment the circle of eager, expectant men who had gathered about them widened a little. Then came the sound—that dull, sickening sound—of a heavy blow, followed by a half-cry, half-groan, and Tucson Joe, the bad man from Bitter Creek and bully of northern Arizona, turning a half somersault, landed full upon his head and shoulders beneath the bar, where he lay white and quivering.

"Quick here, Faro!" cried a score of voices. "Give 'im a glass o' whisky!"

"O sir!" came in a low, soft tone, and a light, shapely hand rested upon the arm that had so summarily dealt with Tucson Joe. "O sir! I am so sorry, indeed, to have been the cause of this. He will seek your life in revenge for this terrible punishment which you have inflicted upon him," said the Kid, in a tone of deep regret.

"Let him seek! And much good may it do him!" replied the stranger. "But see here, my lad. Did you steal his pocket-book, as he said you did?"

"No—no!" cried the boy, earnestly. "I did not. So help me God, I know nothing about it."

"Well, I believe you, my lad," declared the stranger. "But now you had better get out of here. This is no place for an honest man or boy. You had better go, and so will I." And he turned toward the door.

"Say, my lad, are you in a hurry?" asked the stranger. "If you are not, I would like to talk with you a little. The hour is not yet late; come down to camp with me, will you?"

"If you wish me to," replied the boy. "And please, kind sir, let me thank you for the timely assistance——"

"There—there! That will do for the present. But if it will give you any pleasure to thank me for doing my duty toward a fellow-creature in distress, why, just thank away. I can stand it," said the stranger.

"Indeed, sir, I feel—I know—that you have saved my life."

"Nonsense, boy! He did not intend to murder you."

"O sir! You don't know that man, or you would n't doubt it," declared the boy, earnestly.

"No. I don't know him, nor do I want to. I am a stranger here. Do you live here?" queried the man.

"Live here? No—yes. That is, I am staying here," stammered the boy.

"Not living, but just staying," mused the stranger. "Well, I understand that all right enough. I am not a tenderfoot. But here we are. This is my tent; come in." This was said as they reached a little tent just out of town a few steps. "Come in," he repeated, raising the flap which served as a door, and the two entered.

Placing a box which served at once as table, chair and "grub-box" before his visitor, he bade him be seated, while he sat down upon a large bundle of bedding.

For a few minutes they sat in silence. The stranger was deeply engaged in his own thoughts.

By the dim light of a lantern which was hanging suspended from the ridge-pole overhead, the lad had a good view of his new-found friend's countenance. It was a plain but honest face; browned by the burning sun and winds of the mountains and plains of Arizona; a face upon which was reflected the character of a true and noble-hearted man; a man whose friendship is to be valued beyond all price; one of Nature's true gentlemen.

All this the boy saw, for he was quick to read the unmistakable traits of character written upon the faces of men. And deep down in the lad's heart he felt that he had found a true friend—a man in whom he could place all confidence, to whom he could go for help, if need be; and, judging from what we have already seen, we must needs believe that there would be plenty of need.

CHAPTER IV

THE STRANGER'S EYES STRIKE DEEP.

Presently, as if feeling the keen, wishful gaze bent so inquiringly, so earnestly upon him, the stranger raised his eyes and met those of the Kid. For a moment their eyes met, and the Kid looked down into the fathomless depths of the keen, gray eyes of his companion.

Straight into the lad's dark-blue eyes the stranger looked, as if reading there the inmost secrets of his heart. Unconsciously the lad's eyes drooped before the keen, questioning gaze bent so inquiringly upon him, and a painful blush tinged his fair young face. It seemed to the lad that those keen, gray eyes were looking down into his very heart—so keen were they and piercing, holding him under a sort of mesmeric spell, which he could not, if he would, resist.

"Beg pardon, my lad, for my rudeness," said the stranger, reassuringly. "I was trying to place you. I

"O SIR! I'M NOT AFRAID TO TRUST YOU."

believe that I have seen you before—or, at least, some one who greatly resembles you; but I can not say just where."

"It must have been some one else," said the boy, still gazing at the floor.

"I suppose so. But what is your name, my little friend?"

"My name is—is—that is, everybody calls me Kid," stammered the lad, uneasily.

"Ah! Yes—yes. I understand that all right, my lad. And so they call you Kid? Well, you are something of a child; that name applies very well. Rather young to be 'roughing it' here, I should think. How old are you?"

The Kid flashed a quick, questioning glance into the stranger's face, and, in an uneasy tone and in a voice so soft and low that his words were scarcely audible, he answered:

"Sixteen."

"Pardon me if I seem to be too inquisitive. And so you are staying here, are you?"

"Yes, sir. I have been here about six months," the Kid replied.

"Working in the mines?" asked the stranger with a questioning emphasis.

"No," replied the Kid. "I tried it, but I could not stand it. It was too hard work for me. I have been working at the Casino for a few days."

"Rather a bad place for you, Kid."

"I know it, and I would never go there again if I

could help it; but I ha e to work or starve, and I can't get work anywhere else now," replied the Kid, decidedly.

"I should think that one could find plenty of work anywhere here."

"Yes," replied the Kid, bitterly. "There is plenty of work, but no one will employ me now."

"No one will employ you?" questioned the stranger.

"No," replied the lad, and again his face crimsoned.

"Ah, well!" said the stranger, as he noticed the boy's confusion and his hesitating and reluctant manner. "It may be that I ought not to question you too much; but you look like an honest boy, and, since we have been thrown together as we have, I feel a little interested in you. I may be wrong in my judgment, but it strikes me that you are a little out of your proper element here. Perhaps a friend would not come amiss."

"I will tell you," said the lad, and he raised his head proudly now—all trace of shame and hesitancy gone. "I will tell you why they won't hire me to work. It's because they say that I am a thief, and they won't trust me."

"But is it true?"

"True?" echoed the boy, and his wide, blue eyes flashed with indignation. "True? O God! I suppose that it must be, for everybody says so, and the Judge gave me five months!" And then, burying his face in his hands, the lad burst into a passionate fit of weeping.

For a few moments the stranger remained silent, eyeing the weeping boy as if to satisfy himself whether the Judge's sentence had been misplaced. He was saying to himself:

"A thief? Can it be possible? I never saw a more honest-looking boy in my life. A thief? No! I don't believe it. There's something wrong. This boy has enemies here, who are trying to injure him for some reason."

Then he said aloud to the Kid: "And so they say that you are a thief, do they? What was it they accused you of stealing?"

"Money," sobbed the boy.

"And they really sent you to the penitentiary for five months?"

"Yes."

"And you have been here six months since regaining your liberty, have you?"

"No. I have been here only two weeks since that; I counted that time in. I meant that I had been in this country six months all together," replied the boy.

"Well! Well! If you were the only sinner to be found in this country, it might, of course, seem a little different. But come, lad; don't take it so hard. There's plenty of places beside this. Why don't you go somewhere else? Why do you stay here?"

For some time the boy sat in silence. He seemed to be debating in his own mind as to whether he should trust the stranger or not. Several times he stole a quick, timid glance into the stranger's face, as if to satisfy himself whether he should trust him to the full extent. Once or twice he seemed upon the point of speaking; but, as if his courage failed him, he remained silent.

"My lad," said the stranger, in a low, kind tone, as

he laid his hand upon the Kid's bowed head, "I appreciate your good judgment—a judgment which many older heads lack—in hesitating to confide in a stranger. No doubt there are many people here who, if they only knew and understood you, would gladly befriend you; for there are plenty of honest men here, though they may appear rough and uncouth to you. And if you understood the ways of the world better, you might know where to look for them. But as it is, my lad, you do well in being cautious about whom you make a confidant. Let me give you a little advice; you will find it to be good: Wherever you may go, shun all such men as Faro Bill, the keeper of that gambling den, the Casino, and their associates. They may talk very nicely to you; they may make you flattering promises; and, outwardly, they may appear to be gentlemen. But beneath their fair exterior they are as black as Hades. This may be a little too strong language for you, my lad, but it's a failing I have —I use strong language sometimes. Some day you may know me better; then, perhaps, you may be less afraid to trust me."

"O sir! I am not afraid to trust you now," said the lad, earnestly, as he looked straight into the honest gray eyes of the stranger. "I believe you are a friend to me, and perhaps you can help me."

"Depend upon it, my little friend; I will help you if I can. If you are in trouble—and I certainly think you are—I will do all in my power to aid you. Tell me what your trouble is; let me know all about it, that I can the better decide what is best to do. But first tell me your name."

Again the boy's eyes sought the ground, and a deep blush suffused his cheek. But in another moment this color had vanished, and he stood pale and trembling before the questioner's penetrating gaze.

"O God! I Can't Tell."

"What is the matter, boy? Are you sick?" asked the stranger, anxiously.

"O God!" cried the lad, in evident despair. "I can't tell! I can't! Drive me away, if you will; curse me, as they all have done. But I can't tell; I can't. O God! It is hard —it is hard!"

"You can't tell me your name? Is that what you mean?" asked the stranger.

"Yes—yes. Don't blame me, sir, for you have been so kind. Oh, it is hard to forfeit your friendship now, for I hoped for so much—too much. Let me go, please!"

"Not so! You have not forfeited my friendship, Kid. Sit down and hear me, for I am not done with you yet.

If you have any good reason—and surely you must have, or, at least, think you have—why, just don't tell me. It is all right. But tell me your story, or as much of it as you possibly can, so that I may the better understand what needs to be done."

"I am afraid that I ought not to ask you to help me now," said the boy, doubtfully.

"You need not hesitate on account of your refusal to tell me your name. Tell me your trouble; then I can judge you better. We will then see what we can do."

This was spoken by the stranger in a tone which was kind and reassuring.

"I will tell you all, except my name. And may God help me if I forfeit your friendship!"

"Never fear that, my lad—shake!" said the stranger, and he grasped the lad's hands in his vise-like grip. "Shake! Now we are friends! Now you can trust me —can tell me your story."

"Thank you, sir."

"You can call me Tom. My name is Tom Weston."

"Thank you, Mr. Wes——"

"No—no! Don't call me that. Call me Tom; just plain Tom—that is all."

"Thank you, Tom," murmured Kid.

—:o:—

"She was Prostrated by a Severe Illness."

CHAPTER V.

THE KID UNCLASPS HIS HEART.

"Now," said Tom, "we will hear your story."

"I will be as brief as possible," said the Kid.

"Two years ago my—Mr. John Beaty came here from Kansas. He lived near Kirwin. He was a farmer, and, as the drought and grasshoppers had destroyed his crops, compelling him to mortgage his farm, he was obliged to go away to find work. He and one of his neighbors, James Madison, came out here together. They worked here in the mines all Summer, and did so well that they concluded to stay through the Winter and prospect, in the hope of finding some thing themselves. They were very fortunate, for they discovered a rich mine. Mr. Beaty worked his mine all Summer, and he made enough out of it to pay off the mortgage on his farm. In the Autumn—last Autumn—he sold his mining property for $200,000, and started for home. That was the last we heard of him.

"When he did not come, as we expected, we wrote, but could get no answer. Then we wrote to Jim Madison, but for a long time we could get no answer from him. Finally a detective was employed to look up the missing man, but he could learn nothing about the case. After this Jim wrote, telling us that Mr. Beaty had left there and started for home all right; that, if he had not returned, some thing must have happened to him on the road home. But the detective said that he never reached the railroad, and, as near as he could learn, though no evidence could be obtained of any one's guilt, Mr. Beaty had been waylaid and probably murdered the very same night he received the money for his mine; for he had disappeared that night, and it was supposed that he had gone home.

"We sold the farm to get money to carry on the search, and when that was gone there was but little else that we could do.

"Mrs. Beaty worried so much over the uncertainty of her husband's fate that she was prostrated by a severe illness, from which she died; and I came here to see what I could do."

"Jim Wrote and Told Us."

"Have you learned anything since you came here?" asked Tom.

"No," replied the boy.

"Does any one know your business here?"

"No; I think not—not one."

"And this man, Jim Madison—where is he? Do you know?"

"He was staying at the Casino. He had been staying there ever since I came here till a few days ago. I don't know where he is now."

"And he was there before you were sent to the penitentiary, was he? Did he have anything to do with sending you there?"

"No; I don't think that he did."

"Did he offer, or seem willing, to help you in any manner?"

"No. He did n't know me."

"Ah! You are in disguise, are you?" asked Tom.

"Yes."

"Is this all that you know which will aid us? Is n't there something more that you can tell?"

"Nothing that I can think of," answered the Kid.

"What about this Jim Madison? What sort of a fellow was he? You were, if I mistake not, acquainted with him."

"Yes. I was acquainted with him. Mr. Beaty's folk spoke well of him, and they thought he was a nice fellow; but I never liked him," said the Kid.

And there was a look of uneasiness upon the boy's face as he answered Tom's questions concerning himself and Jim Madison—a fact which did not escape Tom's observation.

"Did it ever occur to you that, possibly, this Jim Madison might have had something to do with the disappearance of Mr. Beaty?" asked Tom.

"Yes—no. I—I don't know. I could n't find out any thing," said the boy, haltingly.

"You think, though, that he might have had. Were you and he intimately acquainted with one another?"

"Yes," answered the Kid. And again his embarrassment manifested itself in a deep blush.

"How long had you been acquainted with him before you came here—or before he came here, I mean?"

"About a year," replied the Kid.

"Why did n't you go to him and ask him to help you, if you did n't suspect him of having something to do with the disappearance of Mr. Beaty?" asked Tom.

"I—I thought that—that I had better not. I did n't like to—ask—to go to him," stammered the lad.

"You don't want to tell me why."

"I can't."

"Ah!" mused Tom. "Here's difficulty. Here's a mystery. There's something about this, or more likely about the boy, that he won't tell me." Then he said, kindly:

"Well—well! It don't matter. But, now, what do you propose to do? What do you want to do?"

"I want to find out what has become of Mr. Beaty," he replied.

"And punish the murderers," suggested Tom.

"Yes—of course."

"The property can be recovered, too, I think—or, at least, a part of it."

"Do you think so?" asked the boy, doubtfully.

"Certainly. You can recover what they have not squandered," declared Tom.

"Would you help me to detect the murderers and

punish them for what property we may be able to recover?" asked the boy, eagerly.

"That would be a pretty large reward, I think. Don't you?"

"No. It will suit me. Perhaps we won't be able to recover any thing. If I had money, I would pay you for helping me; but I have not. This is the best that I can do."

"I would n't take the money. It 's not money that I want. It 's a rather doubtful case, but I will help you. There are a few things, however, which I will need to know. They are connected wtth this case, and I must find out all I can about it.

"I believe that this Jim Madison had something to do with this affair. Now, I want you to tell me all you know about him—just what kind of a fellow he is. I can then form some idea of how to work him. Tell me how he came to be so intimate with your family—Mr. Beaty's family, I should have said; for I don't know that you belong to his family. Tell me all that you know."

"He was a neighbor, and used to come to Mr. Beaty's quite often."

"Was a girl there?" interrupted Tom.

"Yes," replied the Kid. "There was a girl in the family. He came there to see her, I suppose."

"Ah! There 's a little romance attached to this, too. It might be interesting, and advantageous as well, to know if this girl—or, rather, if you were interested in this girl. But you can do as you please about telling that part of it. She was young and pretty, I suppose?"

"People said that she was," replied the boy. "I don't mind telling you that I was interested in the girl."

"Was there any objection on the part of the parents to Jim's attentions to her?"

"No; they were willing."

"And upon her part?" queried Tom.

"She did not like him."

"If there was no objection upon the father's part that would make him desire revenge, that certainly could have had nothing to do with it," declared Tom.

"No; it could n't have been that."

"You say that he owned a mine which adjoined Mr. Beaty's?"

"Yes, and he sold out at the same time that Mr. Beaty did."

"Do you know whether he ever drinks, or gambles, or any thing of that sort?"

"Since coming here, I have learned that he does," replied the boy.

"Are you a relative of Mr. B—but I won't ask you that." And for a few minutes he sat musing upon what the boy had told him.

"Ah, well!" he mused. "There's a mystery here other than that surrounding the disappearance of this man. Well, time will reveal it."

Time reveals a great many things—things that we are not expecting; things that we would not have revealed and things that we would. And time revealed this—the mystery surrounding this boy; and, in doing so, revealed some thing that Tom did not suspect. A very agreeable

"HE BADE THE KID REST EASY, AND WENT OUT."

revelation it was, to be sure; nevertheless it was altogether unexpected. But this is as it should be. For, if we could see—if we could anticipate—what is in store for us, we would see many things coming that we would rather not see.

CHAPTER VI.

A BOND OF FRIENDSHIP AND A PLAN OF BUSINESS.

For a long time Tom Weston sat in silence, pondering over what the Kid had told him; then, looking up, he said:

"Kid, I have a plan. You and I will be brothers. We will fit out here and go to prospecting. I have got money enough to last us for a while; and, when that is gone, I know where I can get more. Now, the very first thing that I want to do is to find Jim Madison. Of course, you don't want to let him know you. After we find him, we will then do some thing else.

"But it is getting late, and you are tired and sleepy. You will stay with me. You will be safe here. It may be that no one suspects any thing of your motive in being here; then, again, they may. I believe that Faro Bill and Jim Madison are watching you, and that is why they want to keep you there. But we will wait till morning before we undertake to do any thing."

He began undoing a bundle of blankets. Having finished making the bed, he continued:

"There—our nest is ready. Not quite as comfortable, perhaps, as you get at the Casino; but it is safer—far safer—for you, Kid. Just pull off your boots and coat and put them under your head for a pillow, and then crawl in. I am going back up-town, and won't return for an hour, perhaps. But you will be safe here. Here are a double-barreled shotgun and a Winchester; though, of course, you won't need them."

And, placing the gun at the head of the bed, within easy reach of the Kid, he bade him rest easy and went out.

It was late in the night when he returned; but, noiselessly as he entered, he found the Kid awake.

"Ah," he said, "you are a light sleeper, Kid."

"Yes," replied the Kid, "I always hear every thing that is going on at night."

"I was up to the Casino," said Tom, "and I believe that I have learned some thing that will throw a little light on this case of ours."

Tom removed his coat and boots, which did service for a pillow, and crawled into bed with his little companion.

"I'll tell you what it is. That little, dried-up fellow that Tucson Joe 'laid out,' you may believe, is just roaring mad. I saw him up there, and he is cussing every thing and everybody about the ranch. I believe that he knows some thing. I think, from a remark he made, he has got a 'cinch' on Faro Bill. He was just cussing every thing blue, and he said if Faro did n't 'ante up' he would 'blow' on him. He said that Faro and Jim—I don't know who he meant by 'Jim,' unless it was Jim

Madison—had to 'pony up' before another day or he'd 'rise pertic'lar h—l,' as he expressed it. Possibly, we may be able to do something with him."

"No—no!" declared Kid. We can do nothing with him. He and Faro Bill are all one. He is mad now, but that is nothing strange for him; he often gets that way. He will soon be over it, and then they will be just as friendly as ever. He knew Mr. Beaty, and I think that he knows some thing about his disappearance; but we can't do any thing with him. He is the worst enemy that I have got in this town."

"Just Cussing Everybody."

"By ginger, Kid! I believe that is what he meant by his threatening to 'blow' on Faro and Jim. Do you think it was Jim Madison that he meant by 'Jim'?"

"Yes; it was Jim Madison," replied Kid.

"Then," declared Tom, "we are on the right track! I will watch him."

"It may be that you can do some thing with him, but I could not. I have watched him, but could not find out any thing."

"Why is he an enemy to you? What have you done to put him out with you?" asked Tom.

"I never did any thing to him; that is not what the trouble is. He thinks that I am watching here to find out some thing about this case. He thinks that I am a detective, No—he will never give Faro Bill away, if he knows any thing about him," declared the boy, very emphatically.

"What kind of a man is he? What does he do here?" asked Tom.

"He is the worst tempered man in this town," replied Kid. "He won't do any thing. He just stays at the Casino."

"Well, I won't keep you awake any longer. I believe, though, that I have got a clew that will lead to some thing. We will follow it up, anyway, and see."

And, turning over, he was soon sleeping.

—:o:—

"Dropped His Cup of Coffee."

CHAPTER VII.

THE KID DISPLAYS CULINARY SKILL—TOM WESTON DISPLAYS WONDER AND A FINE APPETITE.

Morning dawned at last, and the Kid, who had been awake for an hour or more, arose and went out to enjoy the cool morning air, which swept down refreshingly from the snow-capped peaks of the distant mountains.

It was a bright, sunny, beautiful morning. The sky was perfectly cloudless, with that peculiar murky, hazy appearance which indicates a hot, sultry day. The air had now become perfectly calm. Nothing in Nature seemed to stir—not even a leaf or blade of grass; and, save only the hum-drum of the already busy town, not a sound fell upon the ear to break the monotony of that dead silence.

The sun, just peeping above the eastern hills—or, rather, mountains—bathed the diversified landscape of barren hills and sandy plains in his shimmering rays of golden light, which were fast chasing away the dark and gloomy shadows from their nooks in the valleys.

"Ah! Watching the sunrise, Kid?" came in a low and kindly tone from behind him.

"Yes," replied the boy, turning toward the tent just as Tom made his appearance.

"Well, how do you feel this morning, Kid?" asked Tom, holding out his hand toward the lad.

"Quite well, I thank you, Tom; and how do you

feel?" rejoined the Kid, placing his small and shapely hand, so soft and white, in the broad and brawny palm of his friend. Such a little hand it appeared, as it rested so confidingly there!

"If you will show me where to get things, Tom, I will prepare breakfast. I would like to do some thing for you in return for your hospitality. I am a fairly good cook," added the Kid, modestly.

"All right, my lad," assented Tom, eagerly. "Not a thing could suit me better. Cooking is the bane of my life. I hate it! Beside that, I am the poorest cook on earth —or in Heaven."

After this frank admission of his dislike of cooking and his lack of efficiency in this great art, Tom

BARREN HILLS AND SANDY PLAINS.

set about showing the Kid where to find every article of which his mode of life and limited household permitted the use. The larder furnished enough for their immediate wants.

In an incredibly short time the Kid's dainty little hands had rearranged and put every thing in "apple-pie" order, and had a deliciously cooked meal spread upon the top of the "mess-box" which served as a table.

Fresh venison, which bespoke the hunter's skill, as well as quail, and the lightest and most toothsome biscuits that it had been Tom's good fortune to partake of since leaving the table of his cherished mother, followed by coffee just to his taste. These comprised the morning repast.

"By jingoes! Kid, you are a treasure!" exclaimed Tom, gleefully. "If you were only a girl, now——"

But Tom stopped short of what he would have said; for, glancing across the table at the crimson cheeks of his little companion, who had, in his confusion, dropped his cup of coffee, Tom crammed the half of a biscuit into his mouth and let on as if he did not notice the boy's agitation.

"By thunder! Kid, these are the most delicious biscuits I have ever tasted!" declared the mystified Tom, who was still endeavoring to conceal his surprise at the Kid's strange behavior.

"One would think, by your actions, that you were not accustomed to eating very good bread," said the boy, busying himself in arranging the table, in order to conceal his confusion.

"Fact, too, Kid!" declared Tom, emphatically. "I am the poorest cook imaginable. Slapjacks and sowbelly is all that I know how to cook."

"I don't wonder, then, that you get tired of your own cooking," declared the lad, no little amused by his good friend's rather limited culinary accomplishments.

"You are no novice in this line of business, Kid," declared Tom. "Where did you learn to cook?"

"All I know about cooking I learned at home," said the suddenly developed *chef*, intently engaged with a slice of venison.

"Tell you what, Kid," exclaimed Tom, abruptly. "I have been prospecting for two months up north of here, in the mountains, and I have struck a lead which, I am confident, will prove to be rich. I came down here for supplies and to see if I could find some one to go up there with me. I don't like to stay alone. You see, I can't cook and do the other work, too. Beside, it's too lonesome.

"Now, I'll tell you what we'll do. Just as soon as we get through with this work here, we will go back there and open up that mine. You can do the hunting and cooking, and I will do the mining; and we will divide the spoils. What do you say? Will you do it?"

"I—I don't know. I am afraid I can't. I would like to, if it would help you," replied the Kid, doubtfully.

"Afraid that you can't? What! Not for the prospect—aye, the certainty—of finding a fortune?" And Tom stared in evident wonder.

"I—don't know—I would like to," said the boy. "I will if I can, but——"

"But nothing!" interrupted Tom. "You certainly can, if you will. There can be no question about that. But, of course, we will do all that we possibly can here before we go. We will straighten up this matter. We will next purchase whatever supplies we may need, and go up there and finish my work. I will help you out and you can help me out. An even exchange—see?"

"Yes," said the lad, doubtfully.

"The Bed was Empty."
---64---

CHAPTER VIII.

TOM WESTON, BEING PUZZLED, WATCHES THE KID AND DOES SOME PONDERING.

Six days had now passed since the eventful meeting of the Kid and Tom Weston. Yet nothing had been accomplished. Nothing? No; that is not strictly true. For a close and lasting friendship had sprung up between them—a friendship that was destined to ripen into a still closer union and be more lasting than Tom, at least, had ever dreamed of.

Great-hearted Tom loved the boy with all his heart, and entertained for him a feeling of the deepest sympathy in his almost hopeless task. So brave, so dauntless and persevering, he appealed to the strong man's heart and drew it to him.

But there was a mystery about his little companion that Tom could not solve. Often had he lain still and watched the boy as he went about his work, always with a sad, wishful expression upon his handsome face that greatly puzzled Tom. So slight of form, graceful, and as supple in movement as an athlete, he moved about with step as light and touch as gentle as that of any woman.

"Kid," said Tom, one day, as he lay watching the lad, "I believe that you are the most patient fellow I ever saw. How do you do it, anyhow? I would like to know."

"Oh, I don't know, Tom," he replied. "Perhaps it is because I have learned better than to be impatient. I have learned a few things since I came here, and I also learned a few things while I was at the penitentiary."

"What did you do while you were there?" asked Tom.

"I worked," replied the boy, evasively.

"Oh, I suppose so—of course. But what did you work at?" persisted Tom.

"O Tom!" cried the lad, in distress. "I can't—I—I don't—I can't tell! Please, Tom, don't be angry at me! I can't tell! I will tell you some time, Tom; but I can't now!"

"Why don't you tell me some thing, anyway, and let it go at that? I would never know the difference," suggested Tom.

"What! Tell you some thing that is n't true?" cried the Kid, with an air of surprise. "O Tom! I could n't do that! I won't lie!"

"Well, we won't say any thing more about that. If I ask you any thing that you can't tell—why, just refuse to answer me; that 's all. But without changing the subject very much, Kid, have you ever heard any thing about this phantom horseman who rides in Dead Man's Canyon?"

"Yes. I have heard of it." And the Kid shuddered and his cheek paled.

"Why did you never say any thing about it, Kid?" asked Tom.

"I did n't like to speak of it, Tom. I don't like to tell ghost stories," replied the boy, nervously.

"Do you believe in ghosts?"

"Oh, I don't know. Don't laugh at me, Tom, for I can't help it!" pleaded the boy.

"I have a notion to investigate this phantom business and see what it is, anyway," said Tom.

"Who was telling you about it, Tom?"

"I heard about it today at the Casino. Some one saw the ghost last night. They say that it appears every night now; but, of course, it is all nonsense," declared Tom.

A few days after the conversation recorded above, Tom came home from town late one dark, stormy night, when he had been watching the movements of Faro Bill and his pals, and, after crawling in his "nest," as he termed it, which was made close beside the boy's, and satisfying himself that he could not go to sleep, he muttered with determination:

"My God! He Has Been Kidnaped!"

"No use! I just can't sleep! I may as well go tonight as any time."

And out of bed he got, dressed and picked up his trusty Winchester. After examining it closely, he started for the door.

"Where are you going, Tom?" called the Kid.

"Oh, I am going to investigate that phantom horseman," laughed Tom.

"I wish you would n't go, Tom," pleaded the Kid. "I am afraid. I feel as though some thing will happen. Please don't go."

"Nonsense, Kid! You are nervous."

"I hope that it 's nothing worse."

"It can 't be."

"But if you are determined to go, Tom, let me go, too," implored the Kid.

"No—no, Kid. You can 't go out in this storm. But don't be afraid. Nothing will happen, and I will be back before long."

"But what has started you out tonight, Tom? Have you heard any thing more about it?"

"Yes; but I won't tell you about it now. Wait until I get back. Then I will tell you all about it."

"Tom, come and sit down beside me just a little while before you go. I am *so* nervous. You will think that I am very foolish, I know; but I can 't help it, Tom. Take my hand in yours, Tom; you are so strong and brave, and it makes me feel better." After a long pause the excited lad resumed:

"Do you know, Tom, I believe that phantom horseman is in some way connected with this work we are doing here? I don't know what makes me think so—or, rather, feel so—for I seem to feel it rather than think it; but I do, and I can 't help it."

"I don't like to talk to you about this tonight, Kid,"

said Tom; "for you are too nervous. But I will say this much: If there is any truth in this story—which I do not credit for a moment—it may lead us to some thing or other."

"Then you think as I do, Tom. You believe that it is connected with our work here."

"I don't like to say that, Kid," said Tom.

"Tell me the truth, Tom; don't try to deceive me. I know that you think so; you do believe it," declared the boy.

"Do you feel better now, Kid?" asked Tom.

"Yes. Thank you, Tom; you may go now, if you really must."

"Well, good-by. I won't be gone long."

In a few moments he was on his way toward Dead Man's Canyon. But if the phantom horseman rode that night Tom Weston did not see him.

After walking through the canyon and back without seeing any thing, and feeling a bit conscience-stricken at leaving his little friend alone as he had, he decided to postpone his interview with the ghostly rider and return home as quickly as possible.

Somehow, an uneasy feeling crept over him as Tom turned down toward the grassy plot where his lonely little tent gleamed white and ghost-like in the darkness. Just why he felt so nervous he could not tell, nor why he quickened his pace.

Eagerly, and with trembling hand, he raised the flap which served as a door and called: "Kid!"

But there was no answer.

Hastily lighting a match, he looked around. The Kid's "nest" was empty. No sign of a struggle—nothing to indicate what had become of the boy.

For a moment this brave, resolute and self-possessed man stood bewildered and completely at a loss as to what to do. Utterly confounded, he could neither think nor act.

"My God!" he cried, sinking down on the bed and striving to collect his scattered wits. "He is gone! He has been kidnaped!"

CHAPTER IX.

ONE-EYED RILEY DRAINS A GLASS AND SOUNDS A NOTE OF WARNING.

For some time after Tom Weston's appearance in Las Animas and his rather unceremonious introduction to the "Bad Man from Bitter Creek," he was looked on by some as a sort of hero, while by others he was regarded as a man to be let severely alone.

To say that Tucson Joe was severely whipped would be putting it very mildly. He was completely "laid out," "paralyzed," "dumfusticated," "chewed up and spat out." At least, these are samples of the expressions which the people of the town applied to his case.

"When a man is whipped—why, he's whipped; an' that's the eend on 't," growled Tucson Joe. But deep down in his heart, if he had a heart—and I very much doubt if he had, for he was never known to do a kind act

"It was the Phantom Horseman!"

or say a kind word to any one—he vowed that some day he would "get even" with his vanquisher.

But it is not so much what Tucson Joe said or did that interests us most at present, but rather what some others had to say.

Several days after the little episode mentioned above One-Eyed Riley, the "diminutive specimen" whom Tucson Joe had so horizontally flattened out just before the introduction of Tom Weston, came into Faro Bill's "private office," and, pouring himself a glass of whisky, said, after gulping the "fiery dew":

"Peers tew me, Faro, that ther Kid's picked up a new pard."

"Picked up a new pard? Why, what do you mean, Beauty?" asked Bill.

"I 'll 'booty' ye—ye white-livered, pot-bellied beer tub! I mean jest what I say; an' yer 'll find it out soon enough, too, I reckon, if yer don't mind yer eye!"

"Who is it, Riley—this new pard of the Kid's?" asked Faro Bill.

"It 's that young Hercules as what laid out Tucson Joe," said One-Eyed Riley. Then he shook his little fists and cursed and raged in the wildest fury at his own bare mention of the Bad Man from Bitter Creek.

"I tell yer, Bill, that ther Kid means mischief. It 's my opine that yer have pos'poned his takin'-off a leetle tew long fer yer own benefit, pussonally speakin'. He 's as sharp as ther devil—he is; an' I tole yer all 'long that he needed tendin' tew. 'Stead of takin' my 'dvice, yer 've been harb'ring of him an' a-nussin' him here. But when the right time comes he 'll turn like a viper an' down ye wusser 'n that young gent downed Tucson Joe. Mark my word, Faro Bill: That Kid 'll make yer break yer infern'l neck, the fust thing that yer knows of."

Again the little man flew into a passion and poured forth a tirade of abuse upon the head of Tucson Joe, and finally wound up by cursing everybody in the town, from the Mayor down.

"It appears to me, Riley, that you are a little off your base today," said Faro Bill.

"Off 'n my base!" howled the "diminutive specimen," as, with one gulp, he swallowed a glass of fiery liquor.

"H—SH! WHAT'S ALL THAT RACKET ABOUT?"

"By ther great Horned Spoon, yer 'll be off 'n yer base wusser 'n I are a-fore these many days, ef yer don't mind yer eye!"

"Say, Riley! If you know any thing, tell it. If you don't, you just go to work and find out some thing, if you can. Keep your eye on that Kid and his pard, and see what they are up to," said Faro Bill.

"You would n't b'lieve me if——"

"Hush!" interrupted Faro. "What's all that racket about in the bar room?"

"Let's 'vestigate," suggested Riley, and together the two arose and hastened to the bar room.

Here they found a crowd of excited men gathered about a man who had just entered the Casino in such a state of agitation and fear that for a time he was utterly unable to speak.

"Give 'im a quieter fer 'is nerves!" loudly shouted the "diminutive specimen," who was dancing around in his excitement as though he were possessed.

The "quieter," in the form of a good three finger-lengths of Faro Bill's best "distilled extract of rye," was administered. It had the desired effect in a very short time.

"Spit 'er out!" shouted One-Eyed Riley.

"Yah, dot ish vot ve heers!" yelled Dutch John, the bar tender. "Ve heers dot shtories mit oudt delays."

"Give 'im a nuther snort at ther horn!" vociferated Riley. "A snort of real tarantler juice 'll fetch 'im. Spit 'er out! Spit 'er out! Stan' back, gen'lemen! Stan' back! He's gwine ter orate."

"*It was the phantom horseman!*" cried the excited man wildly. "I met him tonight down in Dead Man's Canyon, and he followed me. Gentlemen, I swear that I saw the ghost of old John Beaty——"

"Take the fool away! He's drunk or crazy!" roared Faro Bill "Out of here with you—you drunken idiot!"

"Got py toonder!" thundered Dutch John. "Ve vants no ghost shtories heer no more! Effry tay soompody cooms him mit here und dells shtories apoudt dose phattum horsemans or soompody vot ish dedt. Py Chiminelli Got, I peliefs dot ish vun tampt lies!"

"See here, Bill!" said One-Eyed Riley, when the disturbance caused by the excited man had subsided somewhat. "I 've caught onto a plan. By the way things air goin', it 's gwine ter get a leetle tew hot fer us here purty soon, unless somethin's did right away. I don't like this 'ere ghost story, but I b'lieve that we kin put it tew some use.

"I 'll tell yer what I carcilate we kin do: Thar 's that thar Weston—he 's heered all about this, fer he 's in thar. Now, I 'low as how he 'll go an' 'vestigate that thar phantom business, but I don't b'lieve that ther Kid will go. Sava?" queried Riley.

"Sava what, Riley?" asked Bill.

"Why, this 'ere, to be sure: We 'll jest watch the pair, an' ef Weston goes out ter see about that phantom business, we 'll go after that air Kid. Sava now?"

"Ah! Yes. But I don't know—I don't know what we 'd do with him after we got him," drawled Faro Bill, doubtfully.

"Don't know what ter dew with 'im? Moly Hoses! Put 'im outen ther way, in course!" hissed the one-eyed fiend.

"But I tell you, Riley, we 've got to be a little careful. We are already suspected of having a hand in the disappearance of old John Beaty; and if this Kid is any of his kin—and I know well enough that he is—and he should come up missing, particular brimstone would be to pay!" exclaimed Faro Bill.

These possible complications seemed to have no terror for Riley, who persisted:

"But we 've got ter dew it. Once we git a hold on 'im, we kin use 'im fer a bait ter trap Weston. We 've jest got ter git rid of that devil, an' we 've got ter dew it purty quick, tew. Cold lead 's got ter settle his hash fer 'im!"

"But how are we to manage that part of it? He 's got plenty ot friends here, and it won't do for us to do it openly, unless you want to pick a quarrel with him and get him into a fight; and I don't think you want to do that!" said Faro, with a chuckle.

"I sartinly don't want ter dew nothin' of ther kind," replied Riley. "But we 've got ter git ther Kid fust. Once we git 'im, as I sed before, we kin lure Weston into a trap. Once rid of that devil, we kin quietus ther Kid. We 'll kidnap an' take 'im tew ther 'Orphans' Home,' an' then lure Weston thar."

"But how are we to begin this thing?" asked Faro.

"I 'll tell yer. We 've got ter git Weston interested in this 'ere ghost story, so he 'll go down thar to 'vestigate it. This is how we 'll do it: We 'll git Jim ter play as how he 'd seen ther ghost—jest ther same as that fool did out thar; fer I don't b'lieve that he saw any thing at all. He jest run that drive on us ter git a snort of whisky. I don't b'lieve ther Kid 'll go down thar, fer he is a leetle bit shaky on that pint, anyhow. Ef Weston goes—an' all Tophet could n't keep 'im from it—we 'll jump onter their Kid an' spraddle out."

"Well, you arrange it, Riley. Come to think of it, I believe that is our best plan," said Faro.

Three days later One-Eyed Riley came into the "private office," all in a flutter of excitement. Calling for a snort of whisky and disposing of it at one swallow, he exclaimed:

"Faro, my leetle scheme has worked out better 'n I ever thought it would. But we've been runnin' this phantom business about long enough. The Kid an' 'is pard have heard all about it, an' Weston's goin' down thar ter night ter 'vestigate. All we've got ter dew is to watch an' be ready when he goes ter bounce ther Kid. Ther last time that Jim cum in an' swore as how he'd seen the ghost of old John Beaty, he jest put ther finishin' touch onter my leetle scheme. The Kid wanted ter go tew, but Weston would n't let him; so we're all O. K."

"You are sure that he will go, are you, Riley?" asked Faro, who displayed considerable uneasiness. "We must be sure of this thing—no mistake here!"

"Thar's no mistake. I saw him start out; he's half way thar by this time. But whar's Jim?"

"Oh, he's with the girls, I suppose. That's where he always is to be found."

"I'll fetch 'im."

Riley immediately set out on his search for Jim Madison. After the lapse of a few minutes he returned with him.

Jim Madison, as we have already seen, was a young fellow and very handsome, though he was quite small for a man. He stood 5 feet 3 inches in stature, and was slim, weighing only 115 pounds. He was familiarly known as "Masher Jim."

The three men soon set out upon their kidnaping expedition. Arriving at the lone tent, where the Kid was impatiently awaiting the return of his friend and protector, and having convinced themselves that he was not asleep, they paused to consider the best plan of action.

"What shall we do, Riley?" asked Faro Bill. "The Kid's got a double-barreled shotgun, and he keeps it well loaded with buckshot, too."

"Bet yer life he has! An' he knows how ter use it, tew!" said Riley. "I 'll tell yer what we 'll dew. I cum prepared fer jest this partic'lar 'mergency. You fellers repersent capital and I repersent brains. Sava? Mighty convenient ter have somebody ter dew yer thinkin' fer yer now, airn't it?"

"Yes—yes, Beauty. You are a regular thinking machine. But let us know what your plan is," said Jim, anxiously.

"It 's this: You, Jim, go up ter ther road, an' then cum a-runnin' down ter camp a-shoutin' an' a-hollerin' fer ther Kid, tellin' 'im as how yer met Tom Weston, an' as how Tom sent yer arter ther Kid, an' fer 'im ter cum with yer quick an' fetch 'im medicine an' bandages an' water, as he 's bad hurt down ter ther mouth of ther canyon. Sava?"

"Bully for you, Riley!" said Faro Bill. "You 've got a head, if you ain't got much of a body."

"Now, then, commence ter wiggle!" said Riley. "Git a wiggle onter yer, Jim, fer that devil of a Weston may cum back. I would n't give two cents a dozen fer yer ef he should ketch yer here."

"All right," said Jim, as he started out to begin his part of the program.

In a few minutes Jim, who was chosen because the Kid did not know him in his disguise, came running down the path to the door of the tent, calling upon the Kid as he came.

"What is it? What's the matter?" called the Kid, frightened and surprised, as he came out of the tent to learn what the trouble was.

"What is it? What's the matter?" echoed Jim, in well-feigned excitement. "He's nearly killed! He's down to the mouth of the canyon, and he sent me after you! I saw him, and he sent me here for some liniment and bandages. Quick! Hurry up, or he'll be dead before we can get back there!"

Without a moment's thought or delay, and almost crazed with grief and fear, the Kid hastily gathered up what few things were called for, and with grieving heart, blanched cheeks and eyes filling with tears, he followed his guide out of the door, where, as he passed out all unsuspicious of treachery, he was seized by the strong arms of Faro Bill. Then the villainous, one-eyed renegade threw a blanket over the captive's head, and he was completely powerless to resist or cry out.

Frail and delicate though the lad was, it took the united strength of the three men to overcome him. For, brave and dauntless as a hero, he fought with the desperation of a tiger. Though he was not strong, the awful fear which seized upon his heart—for he was now fully aroused to his imminent danger—lent more than a man's strength to his slender frame.

"Fool That You Are!"

But vain were the Kid's struggles. Breathless and panting, he was soon overpowered and dragged away.

A carriage was in waiting not far off, reaching which he was hustled in and driven rapidly away.

CHAPTER X.

THE KID IS INSTALLED IN THE "ORPHANS' HOME,"—THE SIREN REPULSED.

In half an hour from the time when the Kid was so treacherously thrown into the carriage, it drew up before the door of a large, two-story brick, just within the outskirts of the town, and known as the "Orphans' Home." It was a low, disreputable dive, kept by Mlle. Laitner—a character which we need not describe.

Here the lad was hurried quickly within, where he found himself a prisoner, shut up in a small room in the center of the building, on the second floor.

Making a survey of his prison, he saw that the room contained but one door, and no windows at all, except a small skylight in the center of the ceiling, through which he might catch glimpses of the sun by day and of the stars by night.

For six days the Kid had seen no one but the "lady of the house," as she styled herself. But now One-Eyed Riley came. He was at all times the very embodiment of ill-nature, but on this occasion he seemed to have no particular business, unless it was to torment the poor lad by his hideous presence.

But the Kid had no great reason to complain of the treatment which he received. In truth, beyond the fact that he was a prisoner and was not permitted to leave his room, there was nothing in particular of which he could justly complain, unless it was the (to him) disgusting and abhorrent attention of Mlle. Laitner to the handsome youth.

MLLE. LAITNER.

"Why won't you let me go away from here, if you love me as you say you do?" demanded the Kid, one day, in answer to some things that the siren had said to him.

"Why won't I let you go?" she repeated, in open-mouthed astonishment. "Why won't I let you go, indeed! Ah! It would be as much as my life is worth—perhaps more—to do that!"

"Do you know who it was that brought me here?" asked the boy.

"Do I know who it was? Why, of course I do!"

"Who was it—who were they?"

"Faro Bill, Masher Jim and One-Eyed Riley," she answered.

"And do you know what they brought me here for?"

"No—I don't."

"You are keeping me here a prisoner. Do you know that I have a friend who will punish you for this? Never will he rest till he has hunted me up, and he will avenge my wrongs. He will punish every one who has been connected with my abduction."

"But I have done every thing that I can do for you," said the woman. "I have offered to get any thing for you that you want."

"Stop!" cried the lad. "I don't want to hear any of your offers. They are all vile, wicked, shameless—all mocking at my misery! Go away! I don't want you nor your shameless presence here to mock me longer! Go!"

"Fool!" shrieked the Mademoiselle, her dark eyes flashing angrily. "Fool that you are!" And she turned and left the lad alone.

"O God!" wailed the lad in despair. "Will Tom never come? Must I stay here in this vile, wicked place? O God! Help me—help Tom!" he implored. And, throwing himself upon his bed, he burst into tears.

—:o:—

CHAPTER XI.

TOM WESTON SUSPECTS THE TRIO OF ODD COGNOMENS, AND GOES AFTER THEM.

For a few minutes after Tom Weston returned and found the Kid gone, he sat with his face buried in his hands, completely at a loss what to do or to think. But it was not long that he could remain thus, for he was a man of promptness and decision of character—a man who could not long remain inactive when the welfare of a friend depended on his exertions. He was quick to comprehend the situation, and just as quick to determine upon a plan of action which would meet its requirements.

Yes—the Kid was gone! And there could be but one solution to the problem that was in the least satisfactory to Tom Weston, as to the cause of his little friend's disappearance, and this was that he had been kidnaped by his enemies—Faro Bill, Jim Madison and One-Eyed Riley.

"Yes—they have done this!" he declared. Springing to his feet, he immediately set out for the Casino, in search of Faro Bill and his partners in crime.

As we have already seen, Tom Weston had made somewhat of an impression upon the minds of the frequenters of the Casino. But tonight he created amazement and consternation when he suddenly appeared in their midst with a revolver in his right hand and a Winchester in his left, and, facing the malodorous trio for whom he was searching, cried out:

"Curse You, Faro Bill!"

THE LIONS BEARDED.   89

"All hands up! Now, mark you! The first one of you that moves a hand will be bored so full of holes that his dirty hide won't hold whisky! I have a little business to settle with you three fellows."

Apparently without moving a muscle other than the organs of speech, he addressed these words to the bystanders:

"I Have a Little Business to Settle."

"Gentlemen, I know these three fellows went to my tent tonight, when I was away, and stole my boy—the Kid. They are the only enemies that the Kid has. No one else would do this trick; no one else would have had any object in doing it. These curs have such an object, and it was to save their worthless skins that they have spirited away the boy."

Hoarse with fury, Tom addressed his closing remarks to the proprietor of the Casino, who cowered before his scornful gaze:

"Faro Bill, hear me! Just as sure as there is a God

in Heaven—just as sure as the sun rises and sets—if you harm a hair of that boy's head or injure him in any way, much or little, I swear before this people and before God that I will wreak a vengeance on you that will make the very imps of Hades green with envy! Curse you, Faro Bill! I will make you an especial object of my vengeance! Curse you! I will hunt you to the ends of the earth! You can't escape me! Don't try to buoy up your fickle courage with such a vain hope! I know, just as well as if I had seen you do it, that you three fellows are guilty!"

"Search the house," cried Faro Bill, "and if you find him, then shoot us, if you want to. But——"

"Search nothing!" interrupted Tom. "You would not dare to bring him here, for you knew full well that I would come here in search of him. Oh, no; you need not think to throw me off the track by any such clumsy scheme as that. No—no; you can't do it, I assure you. I did not expect to find the Kid here. I simply came here to ask you to restore him to his liberty, and I give you a chance to do it. If between this and morning the lad returns, all right; if he does not, I swear by all the devils in the infernal regions that I will make you most wofully rue the day that you committed the deed!"

"I tell you, Tom Weston, that I know nothing about that boy! If I had wanted to make away with him, I could have done it long ago. He had been staying here for several months before you came here," declared Faro Bill.

"That won't do, Faro Bill!" exclaimed Tom. "Since

I came here things have changed a little. That makes all the difference in the world, you see. You know well enough where the Kid is."

"I don't know any thing of the kind! And I swear that I won't allow any man to come here and accuse me of any such a thing as——"

"Keep cool—keep cool, my friend! Your threats are unnecessary. I am here, and you will not attempt to put me out. I will make all the accusations that I want to, and I not only repeat what I have said, but more. I swear that you and Jim Madison, there, murdered old John Beaty, one dark night, down in Dead Man's Canyon! Oh, yes—you did! And the day is not far distant when you shall suffer for it. I know all this, though I can't prove it as yet; but I will. I know, too, that a man who was the poorest and lowest pimp in town one day became suddenly rich, and I know how it was done. I know, too, that a man so low in the scale of humanity that he will serve the infamous brothels of the town as a procurer, luring young people to destruction, is none too good to murder an old man for his money. All these things have you done!"

With this parting shot, Tom Weston turned around and walked out of the Casino.

—:o:—

CHAPTER XII.

THE KID'S GOOD FRIEND IS HOT ON HIS TRAIL.

Back to his tent went Tom Weston, and after disguising himself he returned to that moth-luring candle—the Casino. Here he mingled with the crowd, in the hope of picking up a clew to guide him in his search for his little friend. He could learn nothing, however, save the fact that Faro Bill and his two partners in crime had become terribly worked up by the scathing denunciation and awful threat which he had publicly poured upon them.

For six days Tom had exerted his utmost energy in the task of finding his lost companion, but as yet not a trace of him had been found.

But Tom Weston was not a man to despair; for, as soon as one day's fruitless search was ended, he immediately began plans for the next. Thus for six long and dreary days of doubt and uncertainty he kept up his unrelaxing search.

It was about this time that Tom, returning from a jaunt into the country, one night, was passing slowly along the road just opposite the brick house known as the "Orphans' Home." Pausing there for a moment, he scanned the dim outlines of the structure.

But Tom Weston was not a man who frequented such places, nor had he a thought of it now; but, just as he turned to move on, a carriage which had been standing

"O TOM!" CRIED THE BOY.

at the door and unnoticed by Tom came dashing by him and drove away swiftly.

"Ah!" muttered Tom. "That is Faro Bill's outfit. What can be his business here? By jinks, now! It may be that the boy is in there! If he is—ah, I will see!"

Entering the house, he found himself in a large room which served in the dual capacity of bar and reception room. He was welcomed by a tall and graceful woman, who advanced toward him and bade him enter the dance hall, where the young people were making merry.

"I claim this gentleman by right of discovery," exclaimed a handsome, dark-eyed senorita, seizing Tom by the arm as he entered the hall.

"Ah, Signor! You are a stranger. Beg pardon! I thought I knew you—I——"

"Never mind," interrupted Tom. "I would like to talk with you, if you will be so kind as to permit."

"Thank you, Signor. I will permit. Do you ever dance?"

"No—never learned."

"But I will teach you, Signor."

"No—no; not now. I have come here in search of a friend. I was told that he was here, and I want to find him, as I have some important business with him. If you will assist me, I will give you money."

"Ah, Signor!" exclaimed the girl, eagerly. "You do tempt me. You know our weak points. But who is this friend? What do you want me to do?"

"Can I trust you?" asked Tom, doubtfully.

"Trust *me?* Ah, Signor! You don't know me, or you

would not ask me that. Oh, I would like to be honest; I would like to be good! But this is not answering you. I see that you are impatient. Si, Signor, you can trust me. When Inez Alvarez does this (and she placed her small, jeweled hand in his) she is your friend, and she would die before she would betray you."

"Thank you," said Tom; and he told her frankly of his mission there that night, and what had directed his suspicions to the place.

"Ah, me!" exclaimed the girl, indignantly. "And so the Mademoiselle's become a jailer? I understand it all now."

"Understand what?" he asked. "Tell me, and I will give you gold for telling me."

"Si, Signor, You Can Trust Me."

"But you will not betray me?"

"Betray you? Heavens—no! I will swear it, if you want me to," he declared.

"No—no; not that. I am not afraid to trust the man that 'laid out' Tucson Joe. A man so brave and strong must be noble and true. But I don't know anything. I only suspect, and I want to tell you why. We have rules here that all must obey, and, if you were acquainted with us, you would know. I can't go with you, but here is a card with the number of my room. The second door beyond mine is occupied by some one, I think. I have seen the Mademoiselle go there. She don't allow any of us to go there. The forbidden room adjoins her own, and the next one beyond this is locked up. So there is no one near this room but herself. This is all that I can tell you."

"Thank you," said Tom, as he placed some gold pieces in her hand.

"Thanks—thanks," whispered the girl, warmly. "And may you not forget the little Spanish girl who, perhaps, has almost risked her life to befriend a stranger. Come; I will show you the way." She led him to the hall at the foot of the stairs, and, extending her hand, said: "I can go no farther. Adios."

"Good-by," answered Tom as he ascended the stairs.

"This is the place," mused Tom, as he paused before the door to which he had been directed, and, placing his broad shoulder against it, he quickly forced it open.

As he entered the Kid sprang from the bed on which he was lying, but in the darkness he was unable to recognize his rescuer.

"Who is this?" demanded the Kid.

"H—sh! It is I—Tom."

"O Tom!" cried the grateful Kid. In a moment he felt himself clasped in the close embrace of his great, strong, noble-hearted friend, and his slight and yielding form was pressed to the strong man's heart.

With a feeling of unspeakable joy, the lad, yielding for a moment to that close embrace, whispered:

"O thank God! Thank God!" And his arms stole around his friend's neck, and, drawing his head down to him, he imprinted a kiss upon the weather-beaten cheek of his brave and generous rescuer.

"H—sh!" whispered Tom. "Wait till we get out of here. Come, my lad." Together they went down the stairs and out into the night.

Hardly had they reached the road when they saw that there was a commotion in the house, and Tom was not slow in divining the cause.

"They have discovered our flight," said Tom, in triumphant glee.

"O Tom! I knew that you would come for me."

"Of course you did."

"And are you all well, Tom?"

"Why, yes; of course. I am always well."

"But was n't you hurt at all?"

"Hurt? Why, no. What made you think so? Who told you that I was hurt?"

"Not long after you had gone down to the canyon to investigate the phantom horseman, a man came running to our camp from the road, calling me by my camp name. He told me that he had seen you, and that you were at the mouth of the canyon, badly hurt. He seemed to be so excited, when he came up, that I could hardly understand him. But I see through it all now. Oh, if I had only known that you were not hurt, I would n't have cared so much for being shut up there! I was so shocked when the pretended messenger told me you were hurt that I never stopped to think about any thing else, but just gathered up the articles which he said you had sent for, and followed him out. As I stepped outside the tent a man jumped on me from behind, and the man I was following turned and grabbed me in his arms. Then another threw a blanket over my head. I struggled and fought as hard as I could to get my arms free, but they were too much for me. I believe that if I could have got my hands free I could have got away from them."

"I don't know about that, Kid. You are a pretty smart boy; but those three men, all of whom are larger and stronger than you are, would be rather too much for even you."

"Well, I suppose so. But what did you see down at the canyon?" asked the boy, anxiously.

"Nothing at all," replied Tom. "I don't believe that there's any thing in that story. Well, here we are again."

"Home again!" exclaimed the Kid.

"Home again—yes. But we must be at work. I suppose that you are tired and sleepy, Kid; but I believe we had better arrest Faro Bill and Jim Madison tonight. You can identify them as the men who kidnaped you, can 't you?" asked Tom.

"Oh, I know they were Faro and Jim, but I could not see them. There was another one—the one who came to the camp for me. I don't know who he was, for I never looked at him," said Kid.

"But I know they are the ones who did it, and I am going up there," declared Tom.

"If you go, I will go, too," said the boy.

This caused Tom to hesitate.

"Well, I don't know as it 's much use, either. Perhaps we had better wait till morning. We can 't prove it positively, and maybe they won't skip. Just crawl into your nest, Kid."

The lad needed no further invitation, and his example was soon followed by his stalwart protector; bnt it was a long time before sleep came to the latter. Once he raised up and looked over to where the Kid, wrapped in his blankets, was soundly sleeping. Tom was almost determined that he would venture a visit to the Casino, but he could not bear the idea of leaving the boy alone.

"No—I will wait," he said, and fell asleep.

—:o:—

"Where's Faro Bill?"

CHAPTER XIII.

FARO BILL AND HIS CONFRERES FLY THE COOP.

Bright and early the next morning the Kid was awake and up, busily putting things to rights, for culinary matters had received slight attention since the night of his abduction. No article was in its proper place, and every dish was dirty. But it was not long before every thing was put to rights and a warm meal prepared. Meanwhile Tom Weston slept soundly.

"Come, Tom; wake up. Breakfast is ready."

"Thunder! I guess I would have slept all day if you had not called me."

"Here's a basin of water; make yourself ready, and we'll eat," said the boy.

"All right, my good lad. But I wish I had waked earlier. I fear Faro Bill and his pards will skip out when they learn what has happened. Hurry up, Kid, and let us go to the Casino and see if the birds have flown."

Hastily finishing their meal, they set out together for the Casino.

Leading the way and armed with his Winchester, Tom entered the saloon and paused for a moment, looking around upon the few loafers who had already dropped in to take their morning dram. Then, approaching the bar, he demanded of Dutch John in a tone of stern command:

"Where's Faro Bill?"

"Py chiminelli toonder!" exclaimed the cowardly Dutchman. "I toandt know vare he ish."

"Out with it, you blear-eyed bloke, or, by thunder, I'll blow the whole top off your head!" As he said this, Tom slipped his hand threateningly toward the lock of his gun in a manner that convinced the Dutchman of his imminent peril.

"Got py toonder, mein herr! I toandt know. He ish nix heer. He ish gone und avay rooned mit himself off, py chiminelli toonder!"

"We will now search the house and see," declared Tom, "and if you have lied to me, I will try a little target practice upon you. I will fix you so you won't hold beer!"

THE DISHES WERE ALL DIRTY.

"Got py toonder chimeny! Dot vas padt peesness for me," puttered the Dutchman.

"Out with it, then. Where have they gone?" Tom demanded.

"Py chimeny toonder, he rooned avay mit dose One-Eyed Rileys off, und mit Shim, und I toandt know vare. Py chiminelli, I toles you de troot apoudt dot peesness, I shware py toonder!"

The frightened Dutchman was whining. But he had told the truth, for a search of the uncanny premises disclosed the fact that the three had left just as soon as they had been told of the Kid's escape.

Less than an hour after Tom rescued the Kid from the "Orphans' Home" a messenger arrived at the Casino with news of the rescue, and in less than twenty minutes the trio—Faro Bill, Masher Jim and One-Eyed Riley—left Las Animas.

Tom was now satisfied that they were really gone, and that the Dutchman had not lied about that part of it, at least.

"Well, there's nothing left us, Kid, but to go back home and wait. We won't gain any thing by worrying. Some thing will turn up, by-and-by; so let us wait. The vultures are in hiding some where—most likely near by—and if we lie low and keep out of sight, they are sure to bob up before long."

"You know best what to do," said the Kid.

"Here is what we'll do, my lad: We will investigate this phantom story first. If nothing further turns up, after we've settled that, we can go up to my camp in the mountains for a month. I think I can finish my work in that time, and find out just what I have got up there. By that time Faro Bill and his pals will crop out at some point. It may seem to you, Kid, that it will give them a chance to escape; but I do not fear that they will attempt any thing of the kind. All their property is here, and they will not leave that. It will need their attention. Beside, the gang will think, when they find we have gone, that we have either given up the chase or struck a cold trail.

"That's about my plan, Kid. But, before we go, I want to find out for sure whether there is any thing in that ghost story. I don't believe there's any phantom horseman any more than I believe One-Eyed Riley is a saint; but I know you do, and I want you to be satisfied on this point."

"I can't help believing it, Tom. I know that you will think me foolish, but I feel that I ought to go and see if I can learn any thing about the ghostly rider in Dead Man's Canyon. Don't laugh at me, Tom, for I can't help it."

"Be it true or false, we will investigate it thoroughly before we go away or do any thing else," promised Tom.

Thus it was arranged, and in a few days they were ready for their tour of observation down in Dead Man's Canyon.

—:o:—

"THE PHANTOM HORSEMAN."
---108---

CHAPTER XIV.

THE PHANTOM HORSEMAN RIDES BY NIGHT, AND A MIMIC
TRAGEDY IS ENACTED.

The night on which Tom and the Kid had arranged to keep their vigil in Dead Man's Canyon had closed down over the bleak and barren hills, the sandy plains and the cold and dreary mountains, and the scene was dark and dismal enough to suit the taste of the most æsthetic ghost.

The sun had gone down behind the western hills and the last ruddy glow of its receding light had lifted like a veil and crept slowly up the sloping side of a long, high range of mountains to the east of them, painting fantastic shadows upon the dim, filmy outlines of the mountain slopes, which, in the distance, appeared smooth and velvety, as if carpeted with a rich coat of verdure.

Beautiful and grand indeed was the scene, but to the eyes of the anxiously waiting couple it presented nothing of grandeur or of beauty. Indeed, it rather appeared dark and gloomy than otherwise; and, to their vivid imaginations, the deep canyons which furrowed the adjacent mountain seemed peopled with wild, weird and shadowy forms, which flitted restlessly from place to place as the blackness of night chased away the last ray of waning twilight.

They stood before the door of their little tent, looking away toward that black, yawning chasm in whose dark and mysterious depths the bloody tragedy had been committed which placed such an uncanny bane upon the lonely spot known as Dead Man's Canyon.

When the last ray of light had lifted, and the last faint tinge of color, which had flitted for a moment upon its rugged side and limned the cold rocks with its beautiful tints of purple and gold, had given way to the inky blackness which crept up and around it like some mystic spell till the dark canyon had faded from their sight, Tom turned to his little companion and said:

"The moon will be up at ten o'clock. It is eight now, and I think that by the time we get down there the ghost will be out. As a general thing, you know, ghosts like moonlight nights."

"Tom, don't make light of this. You don't know what we may see tonight," said the Kid, and his voice trembled with the emotion which he could not repress.

"What *we* may see?" repeated Tom, turning a keen, questioning glance upon his little companion. "No—no, Kid; you don't want to go down there. You had better not go."

"O Tom! I want to go. I *must*—I WILL go!" cried the boy.

"Well, if you will go, and you think that your nerves are strong enough to stand the strain, why, come along—that 's all," assented Tom.

"I can stand almost any thing now, Tom, especially if it will lead to the discovery of my father's—of——"

"Well, never mind," interrupted Tom. "You have said that much that you did not want me to know. But never mind; it is no more than I have suspected for some time. And so John Beaty, the missing prospector, was your father?"

"Yes," replied the Kid, with down-cast eyes. "There were born to my parents, John Beaty and wife, two boys and a girl. I am the only one living."

"You are a brave boy," said Tom, "and I don't for a moment doubt your courage, but I am not so sure about your nerves. But, come; let us be off." And together they set out upon their mission.

Two hours later they entered the dark, mysterious depths of Dead Man's Canyon—a deep, winding defile, through which, until the preceding year, the travel to and from the town to the south had to pass, but which was now abandoned, so it was said, because of its ghostly visitant.

They had reached a point nearly midway its length and at its narrowest place, where there was a sharp angle in its course, and almost at the very spot where it was supposed that the murder had been committed. Here they paused, standing under the overhanging cliff which towered for a thousand feet above their heads, and impatiently watched and listened.

Said Tom afterward, in speaking of this: "Somehow, a queer sort of feeling came over me—a sort of shivering feeling, as if some thing first hot and then cold was chasing up and down my spine. And then came, as nearly as I can describe it, a feeling like being mesmerized—an irresistible desire to do some thing.

"We were standing thus when, all of a sudden, and as if rising from the ground, not twenty yards away, the dim and shadowy outlines of what we instantly knew to be the phantom horseman appeared, riding directly toward us. I felt that I could not move if I would.

"As the phantom rider drew near, and as he passed by within six feet of us, I could see the bushes and rocks on the opposite side of him, through the shadowy form of both horse and rider. Neither I nor the Kid noticed the features of the phantom. Perhaps we could not."

Passing around the jutting point of the cliff which formed the angle, the phantom, riding at a slow pace, disappeared. Without a sign or word, and as if both were acting under the same spell—impelled by the same power—the silent watchers turned and followed the ghostly rider. A few paces brought them to the point of the angle, whence, looking down the road, they beheld a sight which caused even the blood of hardy Tom to run cold.

Rooted to the spot, as it seemed, and unable to move —stricken dumb with horror—they beheld what appeared to them a horseman riding slowly down the road.

He had just reached a huge bowlder which had fallen from above, and around which there was scarcely room for the horse to pass, when, as he turned the point of the rock, his horse reared and plunged as if frightened by some one rising up suddenly from behind the rock, seizing him by the bridle-rein and jerking him back. At the same time the rider threw up his hands, as if some one had struck him to the heart with a knife, and fell backward. As he fell, the hilt of a knife, protruding from his breast, was plainly seen by the horrified watchers.

In an instant, and as if breaking away from his captors, the horse sprang forward, throwing his rider from the saddle. As he fell his foot caught in the stirrup, and he was dragged after the flying and now doubly frightened steed.

Mechanically, and as if acting under the spell of some strange and irresistible charm, the two friends followed after the fleeing horse. A minute later they saw the horse, still dragging the murdered man after him, turn from the main canyon and disappear in a deep, narrow defile which came down from the left. After following up this defile a hundred yards or more, they again caught a glimpse of the horse. This time he was high up on the side of the mountain. They saw him just as he came out from the dark shadows of the trees; and, as the light of the moon fell full upon them, they saw the man drop, as if freed from the stirrup which had till now held him.

Still impelled by that irresistible spell, the terrified friends followed. Arriving at the spot where they had last seen the horse, and where it seemed the body had fallen, they saw, just as they clambered over a huge pile of rocks, the bleaching skeleton of a man.

It was a wild and lonely spot where they found it. Lying in a little hollow, on the white and glistening sand, it was completely hidden from view until the two stood almost directly over it.

The body of the murdered man must have lain there undisturbed, for the bones were all intact. The clothing had decayed and fallen away, and between the ribs, directly over the region of the heart, a knife was sticking.

It had been driven through the victim's heart by a quick and powerful blow, for it had struck a rib, piercing which, it had buried itself in his heart. As the doomed man fell from his horse and was dragged away, the knife, so firmly imbedded, had been wrenched from the hand of the assassin, that some day it might serve as a witness against the murderer.

"O God!" wailed the Kid, clasping his hands upon his forehead and trembling in his every nerve and fiber. "O God! At last—at last!" And, sinking down upon his knees beside those bleaching bones, he cried as though his heart were breaking.

But Tom Weston, as we have already seen, was a man of nerve, a man of quick thought and action, a man who would not be a long while inactive

"Directly Over the Heart a Knife was Sticking."

—quick to decide upon what to do and how to do it. After surveying the scene for a moment, he knelt beside the skeleton, and, drawing the knife from its long resting place, examined it closely.

On the handle of the knife was inlaid a long piece of silver, upon which was engraved the name of its owner, the man who had dealt that blow of treacherous murder in the dark canyon below:

:...................:
: J. W. MADISON. :
:...................:

"Ah," muttered Tom, as his keen eye rested upon the tell-tale knife, "here's evidence, and it comes almost like a voice from the grave. They say that 'dead men tell no tales,' but this is an exception. And so it *was you*, Jim Madison, who dealt that murderous blow—who slew your good neighbor and trusting friend!"

On inspecting the remnants of the murdered man's garments, a pocket-book was found, which contained a few papers and $100 in gold. The papers related to his business affairs, and they fully and undeniably established the identity of the remains.

"Well—well!" said Tom. "This settles one part of our work. Now for the other."

Tenderly gathering the bones in a heap, he covered them over with stones, to protect them until he could give them Christian burial. He then raised the weeping Kid to his feet, handed him the pocket-book and papers, and led him away.

Back into the deep and dark canyon they went again, and sadly and slowly retraced their steps homeward.

For them, the mystery of Dead Man's Canyon was solved. They felt—aye, they knew—that the phantom horseman would ride no more.

Again at their solitary tent, sad and weary though they were, they felt that now they were prepared to take immediate and decisive action against their enemies.

"It only remains for us to find them," declared Tom, triumphantly, "and that we will do."

CHAPTER XV.

THE KID MAKES PROGRESS IN THE ACCOMPLISHMENT OF A VOW AT HIS MOTHER'S GRAVE.

It was late the next morning—or, rather, the same morning, for they were up far beyond midnight—when Tom and the Kid awoke, after a short but refreshing sleep. The sun was fast climbing toward the zenith and the hum of the busy town greeted their waking ears.

Arising from their hard beds, Tom went about making a fire, while the Kid began his preparations for their breakfast. Necessarily, such preparations were very simple; for camp life in the wild and semi-barbarous mountain regions of Arizona did not, at that period, permit an elaborate display of either cooking or household equipments. On this particular morning their stock of provisions was very low, being reduced, as the Kid put it, "to the starving point."

Nevertheless, the Kid set about his task with a light heart compared to what he had hitherto possessed; for the gruesome discovery of the previous night had removed all doubts regarding the fate of his father—doubts which had hitherto lain as a heavy weight upon his heart. The very uncertainty of his father's fate was to him a thousand times more torturous than the knowledge he now had. At last he had learned for a certainty that his beloved father was dead and beyond the power of all his enemies to torment him. The lad's mind was at rest on this particular point.

"They Halted Before the Door."

Beside, the evidence which he and Tom had secured, pointing unmistakably to the murderer, was a long step toward the accomplishment of the Kid's paramount object—the fulfilling of a solemn vow made over the still, cold form of his poor mother who had died of a broken heart of grieving over the uncertain fate of her husband. This was a vow that he would never rest or seek pleasure or happiness in any way till he had solved the mystery surrounding his dear

"TOM WENT ABOUT STARTING A FIRE."

father's fate and avenged his death. The incriminating evidence which he now had in his possession was, he believed, sufficient to convict; and he looked forward with a feeling of impatient delay to the day when he should bring the murderer to account. It made but little difference to him, as he went about preparing their scanty meal, if they were so nearly reduced to the "starving point."

"Well, Tom," said the lad, as he laid their slim fare upon the top of the mess-box which served as their table, "we will have to content ourselves this morning with hoe-cake and that kind of meat which you speak of occasionally."

"Every thing goes with me when I am hungry," said Tom, with a grimace—"even hoe-cake and sow-belly."

"It would n't be quite so bad if we had plenty of it, but we have n't; so we will have to divide," said the Kid.

"Divide 'er up, then, and give me my share," said Tom. "It will stay our stomachs till we can get something more. Lucky it was for us that those villains did not find your father's remains and take what little money he had in his pockets, for we would have had to starve on till we could have earned our dinner," declared Tom as he devoured his scanty portion.

After finishing their meal the two went up town and purchased a supply of provisions sufficient to last them a month or so, and then returned and cooked for themselves a "square meal." It was a tempting vision to their hungry eyes, and to say that they did it ample justice would be expressing it very mildly. They ate as only two rugged, hearty and hungry lads could eat. Tom was loud in his praise of the lad's wonderful skill in the culinary art.

"By ginger! Kid, you can just dish up the best grub out of the least variety of any cook I ever saw."

"If you keep on praising my cooking like this, I will get a poor opinion of you as a house keeper, I am afraid. But say, Tom, what are you going to do next? I can't long remain idle. I must be doing, for I can't rest till my work is done."

"We will not be idle, Kid. We have too much work to do. Beside, it will be cold weather before long, and we must prepare for that, too. This money of yours will last us but a little while; then we must have more, for we can't do much without money. So, you see, we have got plenty to think of and plenty to do to keep us busy."

"Yes—yes, Tom; I know all that. But what shall we do first? I am anxious to be at work. I am willing to do any thing. You understand better than I what we ought to do first. Tell me that."

"Well, I will tell you, Kid, what I have been thinking of—or, rather, the plan which I have laid out. We can't do any thing here now. We have finished one part of our work, and that is all we can do here at present. We would only be wasting time by remaining here, and, as we don't know where to look for our friends, we must wait till they show up. This they will be sure to do ere long if we keep out of the way. But while we await developments in this line, we can be doing some thing else that will help us by-and-by—some thing that will put us in a condition, financially, to carry out our plans when once we strike the right trail. We can't do much without money, especially if they should take a notion to leave here; so, while we are waiting, we can work.

"Now, my lad, this is what I propose to do: We will go up into the mountains where I have been prospecting, and finish my work up there. I think that in a couple of weeks—perhaps three, not more—I can complete what I left unfinished. We will then have money, and can, if necessary, follow those vultures to the ends of the earth. We have got every thing that we need; so all that remains for us to do is to pack up and be off."

"Oh, I don't know, Tom," said the Kid, and he turned away to hide his troubled face. "I don't know. I never thought of that."

"Thought of it?" interrupted Tom. "You don't have to think of it. It's already thought of. All we have to do is to 'git up and git.'"

There was an air of decision accompanying his manner and tone that effectually precluded remonstrance or even hesitancy.

Well did the Kid know that when Tom "set his head to do a thing," if he thought it was right and for the best, he would do it in spite of all creation. This thing he had planned from the first, and the Kid, naturally subservient to the will of others, especially friends, could do naught but yield. So it was arranged that they should start early on Monday morning. As it was Saturday evening, they had but little time in which to get ready; but there was not much to be done, and when Monday morning came the two gold seekers were early on the road.

"Tom and His Companion Set Out for Las Animas."

Three days later, they halted before the door of a neat log cabin, where, for a month or so, Tom Weston had made his home.

CHAPTER XVI.

TOM AND THE KID CATCH A GLIMPSE OF THE SINEWS OF WAR—A RICH STRIKE.

"Home again!" exclaimed Tom, as he dismounted and began unpacking and unsaddling the horses. "Go into the house, Kid, and put things to rights; for every thing is topsy-turvy, of course. It's always so about my ranch, when I have the care of it. I'll bring the things as soon as I put the horses out."

And thus life in their new home—new to the Kid—began in right good earnest.

For several days they busied themselves in fitting up the little cabin and getting ready for "business," as Tom termed it.

Two berths—or "bunks," as they are called—were constructed similar to those of a ship. Tom occupied the lower one and the Kid the upper one. Then, when all was ready, began the long, hard days of toil—toil that led the way to a fortune for the patient and industrious toilers.

For six weeks they worked unceasingly, and apparently to little effect. The cold days of early Winter had come. But one morning when they had begun work a little later than usual, and before a half-dozen shovelfuls of earth had been removed, the crowning glory of their triumphant toil was reached—a rich, gold-bearing lode which Tom knew to be worth a fortune.

"There—there!" cried Tom, as the glittering ore was exposed. "Another part of our work is done!"

"O Tom," cried the Kid, gazing on the glistening quartz, "it won't be long now till we can begin our other work, will it?"

PATIENT, INDUSTRIOUS TOILERS.

"Not long, Kid; and, when we do begin on it, there will be nothing to hinder us from going ahead with it. We will get ready just as soon as we can and return to Las Animas with the news."

In another day their claims were staked out and every thing prepared for the coming of the eager, excited crowds which they knew would come when the announcement of the discovery of the rich find was made.

Monday morning, just as the sun, bright and clear, was peeping above the eastern range of mountains, glinting his luminous rays across the frost-laden earth, besparkling it with myriads of glittering gems, Tom and his little companion set out for Las Animas.

The morning air was cool and invigorating and their spirits high, for the bright prospects of future success in carrying out their work of vengeance were now, by the discovery which they had just made, doubly assured, and they pressed forward eagerly upon their journey.

"You see now, don't you, Kid, that we will gain by coming here?" asked Tom, "even if it has delayed the completion of your work, which I very much doubt. We have the means now, or will have in a few days, and nothing on earth can prevent us from following those villains and bringing them to book."

"Oh, I knew that you were doing the very best that you could. I did n't mean to complain, Tom; and, if ever I showed by act or word that I was impatient or dissatisfied, I am very sorry, for I did not intend. I know that this is the best thing which we could have done. But what shall we do next, Tom? You doubtless have a plan of campaign arranged."

"Planning, Kid, is the least of my troubles, and I *have* planned what to do next. We will go down to Las Animas, and, if we can't get any information about our friends, we will let them go for a while. We will dispose of our property here, and then we can go where we please and stay as long as we please. We won't have a thing to bother us."

"Well, I am satisfied," assented the Kid. "You know best what we ought to do."

And so, as Tom had planned, they hurried on and soon arrived at Las Animas.

Purposely arriving in town in the evening, they immediately repaired to the Casino to learn what they could of Faro Bill and his accomplices. But only one thing could they find out. Faro Bill had been seen in Las Animas but once since the night of the Kid's escape from the "Orphans' Home." He had disposed of his property there and left, and no one knew where he had gone.

Nothing now remained for the avengers but to fix up their financial affairs and begin the search as best they could. This they set themselves about in the manner already planned by Tom. They announced the discovery of the mine, and led thither the fortune seekers.

—:o:—

Ruby Gulch Dam.

CHAPTER XVII.

TOM WESTON TALKS OF THE FUTURE, WHICH CAUSES THE KID MUCH EMBARRASSMENT.

The news that a rich mine had been found up in the mountains spread like wildfire, and by the time the Kid and Tom were ready to return a thousand people were prepared to accompany them.

At evening of the second day's journey they again drew up in front of their little log cabin; but this time they were not alone.

Hungry and weary, the pioneers partook of an improvised supper and then retired for the night. The Kid climbed up to his cozy little nest, and almost before his head touched the hard pillow made from some of his cast-off garments he was sleeping.

Awaking next morning, he was surprised to see, down in the valley which the evening before had been a barren waste, a city of more than six hundred inhabitants. A wonderful transformation scene had been enacted while he was sleeping.

The contention and strife of the next few days beggar description. It would be a chapter of plotting and intrigue—of might against right—and where might too often prevailed. It was a succession of dark crimes, bloodshed and murders.

Here fortunes were lost and made. Some came poor and went away rich, while others came rich and went away poor. But this is the lot of man in all new mining districts.

And so here, in this deep and narrow valley, in the course of three or four months, and before the opening of Spring, had sprung up a mushroom city of over 2,400 souls.

Half a mile above the city, a great dam had been constructed for hydraulic mining purposes. This dam at one point reached the height of eighty feet, and stretched across the most narrow part of the valley. This and a vast amount of other preparatory work had been rapidly completed during the pleasant Winter months, and now, as Spring began and the mines were opened up, the hum and roar of a busy city awakened the echoes of the long silent hills.

DOWN IN THE VALLEY.

About this time, one beautiful morning, when the snow was fast fading from the hills, and along the sunny side of sheltered nooks the first wild flowers of Spring began to show themselves, the Kid returned from a ramble, and, placing a bunch of the flowers which he had gathered in a cup in the window, he turned to his companion and said:

"Tom, they say that the great dam is all finished now, and is nearly full of water. Will you go up there with me? I want to see it, but I don't like to go alone."

"All right, Kid," said Tom, reaching for his hat and gun. "I'll go with you. Come on."

A walk of a quarter of a mile up the small stream brought them to the dam.

Standing upon the top of the dam, they beheld lying placidly before them a beautiful little lake, stretching its shining and mirror-like surface for a mile up the valley and widening out in its greatest breadth to nearly half a mile.

"Oh, is n't it lovely!" exclaimed the boy. "If we only had a boat now, we could take a sail."

"If we were going to stay here for any length of time we would have one," declared Tom.

"Ah, yes! That makes me remember we have work to do. Come, Tom; let us go home. I am impatient to be at work again."

"We will soon be ready, Kid. I have sold our property, and the papers are ready for our signatures to close the bargain. We get $200,000 for it. Now, I will tell you what we will do with our money: Just as soon as we finish our work, we will go to California and purchase a little fruit farm somewhere near the coast, and then—well, I'll tell you, Kid—I don't suppose that I will ever get married. I don't take much after the girls. Of course, I like them; they are all right, and all that. But —oh, well! I don't want to be tied down just yet—that's all. But, of course, you will get married; and then I can live with you—be rich old uncle, you see."

"Oh, I have no doubt you've got it all figured out satisfactorily to yourself; but——"

"What!" interrupted Tom. "Do you mean to tell me that this plan would not be satisfactory to you? A pretty little wife—for she must be pretty—and, by-and-by, one of those abominable little critters that every well regulated bachelor abhors. But, then—of course, I can stand it if you can. Thunder and mud! Kid, what's the matter with you? You are blushing like a school girl! You—well! I'll quit. Come back, Kid; don't run off and leave me. We can talk about something else. The first thing that we must do is to go and have those papers fixed up."

Tom led the way to the notary's office. After signing the papers, they received their money in full.

"Now," said Tom, when the two were again seated in the log cabin, "we are quite ready to begin operations, and we will begin without delay. Early in the morning we will start for Las Animas, and from there we will take up the trail and follow it to the end. Let them go where they may, they can't escape us. They are our victims."

"THE MAN BENT FORWARD WITH THE FLAMING MATCH."

CHAPTER XVIII.

JIM MADISON SUSPECTS THE KID'S RIGHT TO WEAR THE BIFURCATED GARMENT—RILEY'S AWFUL SCHEME.

About two hours after Tom Weston rescued the Kid from the resort which the gang had ironically dubbed the "Orphans' Home," Las Animas was rid of three hard citizens—Faro Bill, Jim Madison and One-Eyed Riley.

Faro Bill had declared: "It's no use; we've got to 'git up and git.' And the quicker we commence to git, the better and safer will it be for us. But the question is, where shall we go?"

"I will tell you where, in my opinion, we had better go," said Jim. "Let us go up to the old 'Mission,' where I stayed last Winter. "We will be safe there, and the boys will be glad to have us back again."

"That's my opine, tew," assented Riley. "Let's go up thar an' stay till this air racket is over. After things cool off a leetle, we kin cum back."

"But there is one thing, boys, that we have got to do if it takes us all the Fall, and this is to find the remains of old John Beaty," declared Jim. "His body must be found before we do any thing else. Not a minute are we safe as long as that knife is left unfound. I know well, whenever his body is found, that knife will be found, too; and it is evidence sufficient to convict us. Tom Weston will search for that body the very first thing that he does. If, by ———, he should find that knife, Arizona would not hold me two hours!"

"It can't worse matters much," said Faro Bill. "He swore that he would kill us if we had any thing to do with the disappearance of the Kid. He knows all about it now, and I believe that he will keep his word. He must be put out of the way. It's the one thing left for us to do, and it's got to be done."

"'F yer 'd a-done 's I wanted yer tew, in the fust place, 'n' laid that Kid away, we 'd a-had no trouble a-tall. But 's 'tis, we 're in for 't, an' I b'lieve as Faro does—that it 'll make no differ'nce 'bout that air knife. Ef it 's so 'bout ther Kid 's bein' ole Beaty's boy, all Tophet can 't stop 'em frum follerin' arter us. By——"

"But I tell you," said Jim, interrupting the vitriolic but frightened Riley, "that old Beaty did n't leave any boy. He is not a Beaty. He 's some 'Smart Aleck' that is playing detective. In old Beaty's family there were three children, all told. Two of them are dead; so there is but one left, and that one is a girl."

"A girl!" exclaimed Faro Bill. "Who knows but this Kid is a girl? What for a-looking girl was she, Jim?"

"She 's a beauty!" exclaimed Jim. "Blue eyes, dark-brown hair——"

"So 's ther Kid!" interrupted Riley. "An' that explains ther racket down tew ther 'Orphans' Home.' Kate, she jes' swore that ther Kid war n't no boy."

"When did she say that?" demanded Jim, excitedly.

"Jes' ter night—when I went down thar," answered Riley.

"Thunder and lightning!" yelled Jim. "Why could n't we have known this before? I swear, boys, I believe the

Kid is Edith Beaty disguised as a boy. She always was, in her actions, more boyish than girlish, anyway; and the old man used to call her his boy. I never could get a good, square look at that Kid, and I always noticed that he acted queer. By—!" cried Jim, with a fearful oath, and there was a wicked gleam in his snaky eye, "I will give a thousand dollars to get hold of that girl.'

THE MISSION.

"Oh, we 've got something beside girls to think about just now," said Faro, impatiently. "We 've got to get out of here, the first thing we do; so let 's be off."

Riley and Jim were of like mind, and twenty minutes

later they were speeding rapidly away toward the old Mission.

The Mission was a large, low adobe structure, built —so tradition ran—many years before by a band of land pirates, who, under the guise of miners and ranchmen, made it their home while they watched the trails leading to the mines in different parts of the country. The band had been broken up, or partially so, at least; but there were plenty of men who would say that the old Mission was still the rendezvous of a band—a sort of brotherhood —of men who, if the truth were known, would soon find themselves behind prison bars or dangling from the scaffold with a rope about their necks. Yet no one could be found to testify against them.

The Mission, like all old places in this country, had many strange stories connected with its history. It was said that many a traveler who had entered there never was seen or heard of after.

It was to this place that the trio of fugitives went. Here they were welcomed as brothers—as, indeed, they were; for they belonged to the brotherhood.

Here for six weeks they had made their home, and in the meantime Faro Bill had made a flying visit to Las Animas, and had disposed of all his property there.

Although, up to within a few days, they had heard nothing of Tom Weston and the Kid, they now got wind of the discovery of the new mines and the great rush to them, for many had left the Mission to go there. Still, they did not dare to return to Las Animas to stay, for fear Tom might return there in search of them; so they had sold out and left there.

Along about the first days of Spring, the brotherhood were thrown into a feverish state of excitement by the news that six of their members who had gone to the new mines had been caught "sluice robbing," and had been hanged in the public streets of the new mining town. This act of summary vengeance on the part of the enraged miners called for retaliation from the brotherhood. Every member of this order was sworn, upon penalty of death, to avenge the death of any member. no matter what his crime may have been.

Now, it was well known to the trio of fiends that Tom Weston and the Kid were living at the new mining town, and herewith sprang up a new hope. They, or at least Tom—for Jim had resolved to spare the Kid for his especial disposal. since he had become convinced that this interesting personage was none other than pretty Miss Edith Beaty in disguise—could easily be included among the ones marked as objects of the brotherhood's vengeance.

A meeting was immediately called, and when all the members were present and the formal opening was finished, the president announced the special business before the house and for which the meeting was called.

In as few words as possible, the business was laid before the house and discussed. Many plans of procedure were offered, but all seemed more or less objectionable.

Finally One-Eyed Riley rose to the occasion and thus addressed his fellow renegades:

"Brothers, I have a plan. I have been a member of this air 'ciety fer nigh on ter ten year, an' I 've seen some things did an' other things as what oughter be did; but this air 's the wust of 'em all, an' it calls fer vengeance.

"Brothers, I have a plan, and it 'll work two ways. It 'll give us vengeance an' it 'll give us gold—millions of it! My plan 's this: Pick twenty men an' send 'em up thar; let 'em put er charge of giant powder in that air dam an' touch 'er off, an' we 'll have a nuther Johnstown flood. What 's easier ter dew? Nuthin'. What then? Not a soul will escape. What next? Thar 's millions of gold thar. Twenty men kin dew ther work in one night and have every thing ready ter light ther fuse by daylight. Then what? The rest of us kin go up an' be thar by daylight, so 's to help the sufferers and rescue things giner'ly. Sava?"

And the fiend's eye gleamed triumphantly.

Every member listened with bated breath to the hellish plan of the demon incarnate. Horrified—almost paralyzed—though they were, yet when Riley had finished his recital of all the necessary details and declared that the crime would be considered an accident, arising from some defect in the dam, not one in all that assembly demurred.

In accordance with the plan, the twenty men were picked, among whom were Faro Bill and the diminutive specimen. Jim Madison was fortunate enough to escape the conscription.

At last the night chosen for the horrible work arrived and all was in readiness. Armed with Winchester rifles, the twenty men stood in a group on the dam. The charge of giant powder had been placed and firmly tamped; the fuse was laid and ready, and the man, with match in hand, stood awaiting the signal to light the fuse.

Presently a man who had been posted as a guard at the town, with orders to return at daylight, returned and reported that all was quiet; that the people, all unsuspicious of danger, were wrapt in slumber; not a soul was stirring.

Dark and dreary was the night—just such a night as befitted a deed so foul. Despite a cloudless sky, the stars, as though shrinking from witnessing such a terrible scene, seemed to fade from sight, and now, when all was reported ready, they were no longer visible.

A better night for the consummation of such a fiendish plot could not possibly have been chosen. And, as if to further aid and shield the demons in their work, the wind had risen to a high velocity and came down from the mountain peaks through the deep canyons with a rush and roar sufficient to drown all sounds made by the demon workers.

The man, watch in hand, stood ready, and at a signal from the captain stepped quickly forward and stooped down to light the fuse which, in a moment, would convey the spark to the mine, and then, as the dam would give way, the mad rush of waters would hurl itself upon the sleeping city.

A moment more, and all would be over. The men had already begun to move away, when, for a moment, the flare of the lighted match lit up the scene. The man bent forward and stretched out his hand with the flaming match to light the fuse.

CHAPTER XIX.

TOM AND THE KID SAVE A TOWN—THE FORMER MAKES A MOST STARTLING DISCOVERY.

The next morning after Tom and the Kid had visited the dam and, later in the day, had disposed of all their mining claims for $200,000 cash, they set out again for Las Animas, fully prepared and equally determined to take up the trail of the murderers and pursue them to the end.

In two days they reached Las Animas, but were disappointed on learning that none of the men whom they were seeking had been there for some time. Dutch John had been there until within a few days, but he, also, had departed, and no one knew where he had gone. But in the course of the day enough was learned to convince Tom that the fugitives had been, up to within the past few days, sojourning at the Mission.

"It's risky, Kid," declared Tom, "but I can see no help for it. We must go up there."

And they went up to the Mission.

Neither Tom Weston nor the Kid, as we have repeatedly seen, was to be deterred from entering upon any undertaking because there was danger connected with it. And now they set their faces toward the old Mission as fearlessly and unhesitatingly as though no danger was to be encountered there.

"We will encounter danger, no matter where we go," said the Kid. "We will expect danger there, and, for

"On They Urged Their Foaming Steeds."

this reason, we will be the better prepared for it. Perhaps we are less liable to get hurt there than elsewhere."

Fortunately, this proved to be the case. Still, they were very guarded in their movements when, the following evening, after a long, hard day's ride, they entered the outskirts of the Mission.

Riding up to within a few hundred yards of the town, they camped. After eating supper, they leisurely strolled up to the Mission.

It was dark now, and little about the place could be seen distinctly; but Tom had been there before, and he knew just where he wanted to go. He had no difficulty in finding the old adobe structure, which was made to serve every purpose of a public nature—reputable and disreputable. Under the latter head, it was used by the brotherhood as an incubator for criminal plottings.

Just as they approached the Mission, a man came out of the door and walked hastily away. His appearance and actions scarcely attracted Tom's attention, but as he turned from the door a piece of paper which had been carelessly thrust into his pocket and which had been drawn out as the man removed his hand was seen by the ever-watchful Tom to flitter for a moment and fall to the ground.

Quickly Tom stooped and picked up the bit of paper. It was addressed to Jim Madison. In a whisper he exclaimed:

"By thunder! Kid, see! We are on the right track now! Come in here, and let us see what is in this note."

On entering the bar room, Tom was greatly surprised

at seeing it nearly deserted. Not a half-dozen people were there.

"Some thing is up—mischief is afloat," mused Tom. "The boys are out on some kind of an expedition, or we would surely find them here. But the note—let us read it." It ran:

"HEARTS' NEST.

"DEAR JIM: Meet me tonight at my place. The boys are all away. They have gone, you know, up to the new mines, and John has gone with them. Tonight, you know, is the night set to blow up the dam. It is lucky you did not have to go with them. John told me all about it. He says that they will blow it up just at daylight. So, you see, you will have plenty of time to stop an hour or so with me before you will have to star up there. You don't need to get there till daylight. Be sure to come.

"Yours on the Q. T.,   LOLA."

Without a sign of the intense emotion which he felt at the horrible revelation of the note, he folded it quietly and placed it in his pocket. Giving the Kid a significant look, he started for the door.

As soon as they had reached the street, he seized the Kid's arm in his iron grip and whispered:

"Quick, my lad! Back to our camp!"

As they hurried along, Tom acquainted his companion with the contents of the note.

"O my God!" cried the terrified boy. "What shall we do? O Tom, we can never get there in time to save them!"

"We must!" answered Tom.

"But it's nearly sixty miles, and we have ridden our horses hard all day. O God, help us! The critters can never make it!"

"But they shall!" said Tom. "There is no alternative; they shall do it."

By this time they had reached their camp. Hastily replacing the saddles on their already tired horses, they mounted and rode away swiftly, leaving every article of luggage except their guns.

It was ten o'clock when they set out on their "race for life." On—on they dashed over hill and dale, traversing now a thickly studded forest, and next galloping over a plain.

Still onward they urged their jaded and foaming steeds. Two hours had passed, and still they pressed forward.

Now they had come within sight of a high ridge—an elevation which they knew to be half-way. Its dim outline showed against the sky, and, though it appeared to be close by, it was several miles away; for when at last they reached its summit it was long after midnight.

Here they dismounted. "We will stop a little while and let our horses breathe," said Tom. "Half the distance is covered, but the roughest part of the road is yet before us. I know a short cut across that will save us about five miles, and I think we can gain time by going that way. Come on."

Both remounted and dashed away again.

Leaving the road, they followed along the ridge for several miles; then they turned down toward the valley. They urged their panting horses swiftly on over the uneven ground—at times in the open, again through the timber.

"Look, Tom!" exclaimed the Kid, as they dashed down into the valley. "Here we are at the river, and it is up out of its banks!"

"We can cross it all right," declared Tom.

"We *must* cross," cried the dauntless lad, dashing fearlessly forward.

"We can make it," said Tom. "Our horses are both good swimmers. Hear! Give me your halter rope. I will tie your horse to my saddle. There, now! We will go together, whether it be to the other side or to eternity."

Fearlessly they entered the water and struck boldly out for the other side. Wading for some distance, they finally reached deep water, and their horses began swimming.

Slipping off their horses to allow them more ease in swimming, they clung to their saddles and swam alongside their faithful steeds.

So dark was the night that it was impossible to see whither they were going. Nothing but the raging and foaming wilderness of waters about them could be seen, yet the direction of the current guided them across. At last, though it seemed a long time to the anxious friends, they reached the opposite shore, and, for a moment, paused to rest their horses.

"Now," said Tom, "commences the hardest part of the road. But we can make it—we *will* make it."

And, addressing a few words of cheer to their horses, they remounted and pressed on again.

On and up the steep mountain side, anon dismounting and leading their horses around some obstruction, again running alongside in order to lighten their load for a spell, then mounting and dashing away at a break-neck speed down some steep declivity or through some open space.

At last, their horses quivering in every limb from the fatiguing strain consequent upon that long and steep ascent, they reached the summit of the range just west of the new mining town of Ruby Gulch as the camp was called.

Catching a few long breaths here, they rushed down the steep mountain side. Now dismounting to lead their horses around a dangerous rock and then remounting, they dashed away again.

On they flew till, within a half-mile of the dam, they emerged from the forest into the main road just three-quarters of a mile from town.

"Kid!" sung out Tom, whose horse was now lagging behind, "My horse is failing. Check up a little, and we will give him time to get his wind."

But the noble animal was almost beyond breathing. Scarcely had Tom ceased speaking when, staggering for a moment, as if striving to obey his master even in death, the noble brute fell—to rise no more.

"Ride, Kid! Ride on and give the alarm. I will go across to the dam, and see what I can do. Ride through the town and call the people out. Tell them to flee to the hills. If they have n't broken the dam by the time I get there, you will hear my gun speaking. If you hear me, gather a few men and bring them up. Be quick, my lad!"

But the noble lad needed no urging. Putting spurs to his horse, he dashed away, and soon disappeared from view.

Tom Weston was as strong and as swift of foot as he was brave, and in an incredibly short time he had made his appearance in the deep, narrow valley just below the imperiled dam.

As he turned down into the gulch from the ravine which he had been following, and scarcely twenty yards below the foot of the dam, he beheld a sight which sent a thrill of despair to his heart.

Brave and dauntless man though he was, his heart sunk with a feeling of horror. But it was for a moment only. Before him he saw the great dam, towering like a huge wall eighty feet above him. He saw the outlaws moving rapidly across the dam toward the opposite side. One man only remained. And just as Tom turned into the gulch below, this man, with a lighted match in his hand, stooped down and stretched his hand out to light the fuse.

For a moment the flare of the match lit up the scene, and Tom plainly saw the man's features—the features of Faro Bill.

Just as the hand reached out to light the fuse, Tom's keen eye glanced along the barrel of his deadly Winchester and his finger pressed the trigger.

A blinding flash, a deafening report, followed by a wild, shrill scream of mortal terror, and the man on the dam sprang into the air and fell with a dull, sickening thud upon the jagged rocks eighty feet below.

Again and again rang out that thunderous report loud and clear above the roar of the wind.

For a moment, the outlaws were panic stricken; but soon, seeing that they were opposed by only one man, they rallied and charged across the dam full in the face of that deadly fire.

Twice — thrice they attempted to light the fuse; but Tom's bullet, guided by the flare of the lighted match, stayed the murderous hand.

"Down upon him! Rout him!" cried the captain.

"THE MAN FELL WITH A SICKENING THUD."

In response, they charged across the dam and poured a volley of leaden hail down into the darkness below. Guided by the flash of Tom's rifle, they began to clamber down, in order to reach him.

With a revolver in either hand, Tom waited until they came within range; then he renewed his deadly work.

Dodging from rock to rock, Tom contested every foot of the disputed ground until he had reached the bottom of the gulch, directly beneath the dam. Here he made a stand, firmly resolved that he would not yield another inch. He refilled the chambers of his revolvers and the Winchester with fresh cartridges, and met the advance of his foes with such a deadly fire that, for a moment, they faltered. But for the threats of the captain, who was exasperated beyond measure and loudly swore that he would shoot the first coward who attempted to retreat, they would have fled and left the dauntless Tom master of the field. Having successfully rallied his wavering host, the captain ordered another charge. But Tom was ready now, and he received them with such deadly effect that four of them went down to rise no more.

"Curse the devil!" cried the captain, in very desperation. "Onto him! Rout him! Up with you, there—you cowardly whelps! Charge! I swear I'll shoot the first man that falters! Rout him out of those rocks! Up there with you—you lubberly Dutchman!"

Thus roared their captain. His last remarks were addressed to Dutch John, whose courage was only kept to the sticking point by continuous prodding.

But now, from down the gulch toward town, came a wild shout, and a moment later the Kid, bare-headed and with coat off, and followed by a half-dozen men, dashed down from the road and charged upon the outlaws.

"Charge!" cried the dauntless lad, and, bounding to the front, he discharged his shotgun into the midst of the enemy's ranks.

For a moment they scattered, but, rallying again, they met the charge, hoping by overwhelming numbers to crush them. In the confusion, though it lasted but a moment, the Kid and his men had gained the shelter of the rocks behind which Tom had intrenched himself, and then began a fusillade which in a few seconds resulted in the death of two of the Kid's men. And now, also, the firing from Tom's rifle had ceased, seeing which the outlaws took courage and once more formed for a charge.

"Onto them!" yelled the leader. "There's but five of them, and one's a kid! There's ten of us! Up—every man of you! Charge!"

Again the desperate devils rushed forward.

And again the Kid's double-barreled shotgun poured its hail of buckshot into the faces of the outlaws, and, springing upon a rock in full view of his men, he cried:

"Stand your ground, men!" And again his shotgun thundered.

For a moment, brave men though they were, it appeared that the Kid's men would forsake him. But now the Kid's voice, piercing and fearless, rose high above the din of the conflict:

"For God's sake, men, don't run! Remember the women and children! Remember that you are men!"

Just as he uttered these words the brave lad dropped his gun, reeled and fell. In an instant he was on his feet again, and, grasping his gun, discharged its contents full into the faces of the enemy.

At this juncture a score of men from the town came down upon the outlaws, who, panic stricken, turned and fled. However, the recruits poured such a deadly fire upon them as they scrambled up the steep bank that all except one were either killed or captured. Ruby Gulch was saved.

While the home defenders were in pursuit of the routed and badly decimated band, Kid crawled to where he had last seen the flash of Tom's rifle. Here he found his friend, lying on a rock and endeavoring to stanch a wound in his right shoulder.

"O Tom! You *are* hurt this time!"

"Not very dangerously, though. Are you all right, Kid?"

"Yes. Where can I find some water?"

"Right down there," replied Tom, pointing to the foot of the dam. "Fetch some for me in my hat."

In a few minutes the lad returned with a hat full of water, and just as he had placed it upon the ground beside his wounded friend he fell fainting at his feet.

"Kid! O Kid!" cried Tom. In a flash he was upon his knees beside the prostrate lad.

In the dim light of the early morning Tom saw that the boy's garments were soaked with blood, which flowed from a bullet wound in his left side. Quickly loosening the boy's garment, exposing his bosom and wounded side, a revelation burst upon Tom's astounded vision.

"My God!" cried Tom, starting back in bewilderment at the revelation which the snow-white bosom had made. "My God! *He's a girl!*"

"The Doctor Came Every Day."

CHAPTER XX.

ONE-EYED RILEY PAYS HIS DEBTS—TOM WESTON SURRENDERS UNCONDITIONALLY.

Tom Weston, as events have already proved, was a man equal to every occasion, and he was equal to this. Not long did he hesitate, but with deft and gentle fingers washed and bandaged the girl's wound, rearranged her clothing and then bathed her face and hands with the cool water which she had brought.

The sun was just rising as he finished his task, and now the people from town came crowding around them, anxious to see the brave girl who had done such a heroic and noble deed.

Breathlessly passed the whisper from lip to lip:

"She's only a little girl, and she's wounded, too!"

"Hear, pard! Give 'er a swig o' this. It's brandy." An old man, who had just come up, handed Tom a flask.

A little was given, and in a few moments the girl opened her eyes and looked about her. Raising her eyes to Tom's, she asked:

"Where are they?"

"I don't know yet, Kid; but I will see pretty soon."

"Who's he askin' fer, pard?" queried a by-stander.

"The leaders of this band of robbers who tried to flood the town—Faro Bill, Jim Madison and One-Eyed Riley," answered Tom.

"Jim Madison is not here, nor Faro Bill, but we got One-Eyed Riley all right," said the man, as the guards brought the one-eyed demon forward.

"Take that cutthroat to town," said Tom. "Will some one help me carry the Kid up to the road?"

Many willing hands were offered, and the wounded life-saver was borne gently up the steep bank, placed in a wagon and driven back to Tom's log cabin.

As they arrived at the cabin door, they looked down into the main street of the town, and they saw the excited people rapidly gathering. Wild and awful were the cries for vengeance which rose on the morning air as the infuriated people beheld the one-eyed fiend who had planned such a demon deed.

As the brave girl, leaning upon the arm of her companion, paused for a moment before the cabin door to look down upon that wild and awful scene being enacted in the town below, the eyes of the people were raised toward them, and when they saw her there, supported upon the arm of manly Tom Weston, they sent up a shout which seemed to shake the hills to their foundations.

In a short time the doctors who had been sent for arrived at the cabin, and soon had both Tom and the Kid feeling quite comfortable.

"There, now!" said one of the physicians. "You will get along all right; but I want to tell you, little girl, you came very near being 'sent across the border.' But you will get along all right. We will send up a nurse to take care of you."

As soon as they were gone Tom arose from his couch and crossed over to the Kid's bed. Sitting down beside her and pointing to the vast crowd of people, whom they could see through the open door, he said:

"See there, Kid! There's the last of One-Eyed Riley."

Gently Tom raised her a little, that she could see.

"THE LAST OF ONE-EYED RILEY."

The Kid shuddered as she gazed through the door down upon the people below and beheld, high above their heads, hanging upon an impromptu gallows, the well-known figure of One-Eyed Riley.

"There's one more," said Tom, as he laid her gently back upon her pillow, "and then our work is done. But there's no hurry; you must get well first."

Wearied by her long night's ride, the Kid was soon asleep, and in a little while the nurse, an elderly lady, came.

"Just make yourself at home," said Tom. "You won't have to bother with me, but this little girl will have to be cared for pretty well."

"She shall have the very best care that I can give her, I assure you," replied the nurse, and she did.

For three months the Kid lay upon her bed, only as she was taken up by her nurse. But now she could sit, and for hours at a time, and with Tom's assistance could even walk about out-doors a little. Everybody seemed to be interested in the recovery of the invalid, and each day the doctor came and carried word back to town that the heroine was progressing finely.

Edith was recovering rapidly now, and her short walks in the open air soon brought the color back to her pale cheeks and restored her appetite and strength.

Tenderly and constantly Tom watched over the progress of his wounded companion, and as the days passed and she grew strong and the flush of health and beauty returned to her fair cheek and kindled anew the fire of pride and ambition in her dark eyes, another revelation burst like a thunder-bolt upon Tom's unwilling vision.

"HE PLACED THE THINGS UPON THE TABLE."

Unwilling vision? Yes; it was so. For Tom, because of an affair which he explained later, had forsworn all "sentimental fancies" for the fair sex, declaring that he would live and-die an old bachelor.

Tom now realized that he loved the girl who had been so unconventionally thrown in his company. Try as he would, he could not banish her image from his heart. That sweet, patient face was always before him, sleeping or waking. Those dark, lustrous, pleading eyes, gazing so appealingly into his own, struck deep into his heart and he surrendered unconditionally.

CHAPTER XXI.

TOM AND KID ARRANGE AN AFFAIR OF THE HEART AND RENEW THE SEARCH FOR JIM MADISON.

Three months had passed since the battle at the dam, and it was May 1—a beautiful Sabbath morning. All Nature seemed to be rejoicing at the return of the birds and flowers. The warm, bright sun was creeping well toward the zenith, and the little city lay quiet and peaceful below. The birds were singing their first glad songs of mating, and the wild flowers were nodding their heads before the cool mountain breeze, when the Kid, lying upon her little cot where the warm sun peeped through the open window and danced about her rich tresses and kissed her red lips, where the soft breeze, fragrant with the perfume of the pine and the fir and the blossoming vine, stole through the half-open door and whispered sweet promises in her maiden ears, was awakened from her happy dreams. Opening wide her dreamy eyes, she gazed up into the honest face of Tom Weston.

"Ah, Tom! I thought you were down-town?"

"And so I was, Kid; but it is dinner-time and the nurse is away, so I came home to try my hand at cooking. I will show you how I do it. Are you hungry?"

"Hungry? Yes, indeed. I am almost famished! But what have you got in that great basket?"

"Oh, it's our dinner," answered Tom.

"And so that's the way you cook, is it? It's good, anyway, Tom,"

SPRING'S FIRST BIRDS AND FLOWERS.

she declared, as he placed the things upon the table beside her bed. "Cake and pie, toast, quail, mountain trout, boiled eggs! O Tom! You have got away outside the doctor's bill of fare!"

"Eat a little of all if you want to, Kid. It won't hurt you," urged Tom.

"Tom, I was thinking today what we should do. I am feeling so well now that I am beginning to be impatient to be at work again. But, Tom, how are we to manage? I can't be a boy any longer now."

"I was thinking of that, too, Kid," said Tom, "and I will tell you what I think, though I don't know as you will agree with me. I think that we had better do just as we first planned to do; but it will be two months yet before we can do any thing. You won't be able to work before that. But we need not be idle; for, while we are waiting, we can be doing some thing else, just as we did last Autumn, when we were waiting for our friends to show up. We came here, and in a couple of months made us a snug little fortune. We did not lose any time by it, either. It was the very best thing that we could possibly have done."

"Oh, I know that, Tom," answered the Kid. "I am satisfied with your plans. You always have every thing planned beforehand. But what must we do now, Tom? I can't stay here and do nothing; I will die."

"I will tell you, Kid, what my plan is. You remember what I was telling you about our going to California? Well, we will go there, just as I planned, and get us a little fruit farm some where near the sea shore and build us a home on some pleasant bay, where we can live in peace and plenty the rest of our days. I was to be a rich old bachelor uncle, and you, you know, was to have a pretty little wife and baby. Who could imagine a more happy home?"

"A beautiful vision, Tom, but like the most of such —visionary."

"Visionary? No—no, Kid; don't say that——"

"But, Tom," interrupted the Kid, "I am not a boy! Where, then, will be your rich old uncle, your boy and his pretty wife and——"

"Well?"

"It 's all visionary!"

"I will tell you, Kid. Let us go there, just as we had planned—just as I had planned, for you never agreed to that part of it, though you acknowledged that it would be a very fine thing to do if we could only manage it. Let us go and find a place that will suit us—I know just where there is one—get it and fit it up to suit our fancy, and then, when we are through with this work, we will go there and live just as I had planned, save only this: We will have to dispense with that venerable and altogether valuable head of the family—the rich old uncle. But we can have the rest of the happy family, Kid."

"Tom—Tom!" interrupted the blushing girl. "Wait a little! I want to think—I—I want to talk with you about some thing else *first*. You are honest and true, Tom, I know, and I believe that you love me, or you would not tell me so."

"What do you mean, Kid?" asked Tom, interrupting her.

"We have got our work to do, Tom. Wait until that is done. You have known me as a girl only a very little while. Don't be hasty in this."

"Hasty? I have been with you every day for over a year, Kid."

"But you did not know that I was a girl. Did you

ever suspect any thing of the kind, Tom?" asked the Kid.

"No. But I was a fool. I can see it all now. I thought that you were a queer boy, but the thought never entered my fool head what the matter was with you."

"I want you to tell me, Tom, what your plan is for our work. We must be at it just as soon as I am able to be out."

"That's just what I was telling you, Kid, or was about to, when you stopped me. Let us understand each other now; then we can go to work, knowing just what we are to do. Let me finish my story in my own way. I am a rough and awkward fellow, I know, and I don't know how to do this thing in the most approved style; but I love you, Kid, as honestly and truly as ever a girl was loved. No—no! Kid, don't tell me to stop. But I see that you don't want my love. You——"

"O Tom! Don't be angry at me! You are too hasty —too proud—too quick to jump at conclusions. Don't be angry, Tom! Don't leave me! Every hope that I have in the world—even my life—depends upon your friendship—your loyalty!"

"I am not angry, Kid; and, as for my friendship, you need make no sacrifices. I have given you my word of honor, and I will keep it. Tom Weston never yet broke his word. I will do the work that I started out to do, if God spares my life. You need have no fear of my leaving you because you refuse me—my love. O Kid! I would a thousand times rather that you should refuse me now than disappoint me by-and-by. No—no! Don't stop me! Let us understand each other now; then we will know just what to expect. There will be no disappointment."

"You wrong me, Tom, by your hasty words; and, if I were as hasty as you, I might resent them. O Tom! I did not believe that you could think me so heartless and cruel as you try to make yourself believe I am! I know that you don't have a very good opinion of girls; but because some girl has disappointed you, Tom, is no valid reason why you should judge me so harshly. Girls are not all alike, any more than boys are. Come here, Tom, and sit down beside me; I will tell you why I do not want you to ask me yet. You know, I told you of the night my mother died and the vow that I made. I can't help it, Tom, because you love me—no, I don't want to help it. Never think that, Tom! I can't help it because you love me, nor I can't help it because I love —love you. But I can do this: I can ask you to wait till our work is done—till my vow is fulfilled. And you *will wait*—won't you, Tom?" And those deep, pleading eyes gazed wishfully into his.

"Wait? Yes, Kid; I will do any thing you ask. Forgive me, my brave little girl, for my cruel words! I will not ask you now; I will be content. I will wait till our work is done," promised Tom, earnestly.

"Thank you, Tom; and may God help us to keep our faith in one another. I want you to understand me, Tom. All my hopes depend upon your loyalty to me. I want you to understand why I put you off. Don't misjudge me. I don't refuse you, Tom; remember that."

"Don't be afraid, Kid; I will not misjudge you again. Rest assured of that," declared Tom, vehemently.

"We understand each other now, Tom, I think. Now, when are we to set out in search of our future home, provided we are fortunate enough to live to enjoy it? I hardly think that I should consider this a pleasure trip, for I am not able to work; and, beside, it may help to hasten my recovery, and we may gain time by it."

"We will start just as soon as you are able to go," said Tom. "I think that a change will help you. The journey will be pleasant, and a change of climate is sure to help you. As for its being a pleasure trip, there may be pleasure in it; but it is not pleasure that we are after. Beside, we stand as much chance of hearing from our man there as here. I have offered a reward for him, or any information concerning his whereabouts. I have sent descriptions of him to police headquarters in all the large cities and towns in the West. Detectives will be on his trail, and, no matter where he goes, he is liable to be detected any day. We are almost sure to hear from him before long. But if we hear nothing from him by the time you are able to work, we can return here and take up the trail and follow it to the end. He is our victim—he can't escape us."

"Then we will start in the morning," declared the Kid, "for I am feeling so strong and well today that I know I can stand the trip. But, Tom, where are we going? Were you ever out there?"

"Yes. I used to live there. We will go back to my old home."

CHAPTER XXII.

EDITH TRANSFORMED BY THE MILLINERS—JIM MADISON LOCATED.

Monday morning dawned warm and pleasant, and the Las Animas stage was waiting before the door of the little cabin home when the Kid, with a light heart though feeble step, came forth and bade farewell to the many friends who had gathered there to press her hand and wish her long life and happiness.

Waving a last farewell to her humble home—the home where she had known so many days of suffering, of anxious waiting, of hope and fear, and yet many days of pleasure and happiness—she settled herself down among the soft cushions provided for her comfort and was rapidly whirled away.

Passing over their uneventful yet very pleasant journey, we find them, six days later, comfortably situated at a quiet and highly respectable boarding house in Los Angeles, California.

"We will go to a boarding house," said the Kid. "It will be quiet there, and we will be where we can deny ourselves to persons we do not wish to see. We want to keep out of sight of any one that might be interested in finding us. Such a precaution may be unnecessary, but it is better to be careful. Beside, I wish to remain secluded until I get some clothes. We can't be any too careful, Tom. And now," she continued naively, "your trials are about to begin, for I intend to send for a dress

"She Came Running Down the Walk to Meet Them."

maker and order a few dresses. So, you see, you may expect to have on your hands, for a few days at least, one of those incorrigible creatures for whom you profess such a detestation. Just remember this, and deport yourself accordingly."

"I will hunt me a new boarding place," declared Tom.

"No need of that, for you won't have to be near me except at meal time, and I guess you can stand that—that is, if it don't take your appetite away."

"Well, I can try it for a day or two, anyway, and see," said Tom with a laugh.

Once settled in their new quarters, the transformation act began, and in a surprisingly short time was completed.

It was Wednesday, the third day after their arrival,

IN THE GARDEN.

that Tom, arising from the dinner table, took his companion's arm in his and the two went for a short walk in the garden.

"You need a little exercise," said Tom. "You are too much taken up with those dresses. Lay them aside for an hour."

"But I dislike to be seen yet, Tom. My dresses are promised me this afternoon, and then I can go out. But what is the matter with you, Tom? What makes you look so pale today? I did not notice this until this very moment. What is it, Tom?"

"Oh, it's nothing," answered Tom, carelessly. "I am losing a little of the Arizona complexion—that's all."

"I know better, Tom; I want you to tell me what the matter is. You neither look well nor act naturally. Are you displeased with me?"

"No—no! Kid, you are all right. It is not that."

"Tom, you must call me Edith. You don't like it, I know; but you must accustom yourself to it, so you may as well commence the practice. 'Kid' is all well enough in the mines and when we are alone; but you always forget."

"Yes—yes. I understand, Kid—I mean Edith. But I am afraid that you will find it a hard task to make any thing of me, except Tom Weston. He's whole cloth, Kid; a yard wide and dyed in the wool; warranted not to rip, ravel or run down at the heel——"

"Tom—Tom!" laughed Edith, placing her small and white hand over his mouth. "I won't hear any more! Tell me, Tom, what the matter is with you today."

"Oh, my shoulder hurts a little—that's all."

"Have you had any thing done for it since we came here?"

"No."

"Then you go and have it seen to, Tom," said Edith, reproachfully. "It's a shame for you to be so careless of yourself. You have had a doctor here every day to see me, and not once have you been treated for your own hurt! At this rate, you will not regain the use of your arm this Summer. I bid fair to recover from my wound before you are sound again."

"Perhaps I had better have the doctor examine my shoulder," assented Tom.

"I doubt much," said Edith, "whether it was properly attended to in the first place. Maybe that murderous bullet should have been probed for and extracted at Ruby Gulch. It has hurt you ever since you received the wound."

"When I return from the doctor, I suppose we will need some one to give me an introduction to you; but, then, I guess I can stand it."

For a moment Edith stood and watched the manly form and bearing of Tom Weston as he walked down the street, and then, with a look of pity in her eyes, she turned back to the house.

"I will give him a pleasant surprise when he returns home," thought Edith.

The "transformation act," as Tom termed it, was completed to Edith's satisfaction. When he returned in the evening, pale and so weak that he had to be assisted from the carriage into the house by the old doctor who had waited upon Edith, he was most agreeably surprised at the beautiful and graceful young lady who came running down the walk to meet him.

"Don't touch my arm, Edith," said Tom, in a warning tone. "I had that bullet taken out."

"I was afraid you would have to endure that operation, in order to be cured."

"Yes; it's over with now. My doctor says I am sure

to be myself again some day." And the brave sufferer lay down on the sofa and turned his admiring gaze upon the beautiful vision before him.

"Poor Tom!" softly whispered Edith, brushing his brown locks from his broad, pale forehead. "What a shame that this was not done in the first place!"

"Stand out there, Kid, in the middle of the room, and let me have a good, square look at you, and I will promise never to be so negligent again."

"Will you also promise to call me Edith?" she asked, as she complied with his request.

"By thunder! Kid—I mean Edith—you are the pret——"

"Tom!" cried the girl, stopping his mouth with both her hands. "Stop, sir! I won't have any of your flattery. For shame, Tom, to turn flatterer! But really, now, is n't a girl almost as nice as a boy?"

"Some girls are," he acknowledged, but reluctantly. "But say, Kid! I have got some news that will interest you, I think."

"What is it, Tom?"

"I got an answer to our advertisement for Madison. He is in San Francisco. I got a letter from a private detective there, stating that he had seen and located our man, and he wants us to come on there and arrest him just as soon as possible, as he fears that he may leave."

"And you are all crippled up so you can't go for a while," sighed Edith.

"But we will go, Kid; we will start with tomorrow's sunrise." In the morning they left for the Sunset City.

"What He Saw."
---180---

CHAPTER XXIII.

TOM SPOILS JIM MADISON'S PLAN OF MURDER, BUT THE LATTER RECAPTURES EDITH.

"Py chiminelli Got!" exclaimed Dutch John, on the night of the fight at the dam, as the Kid and his men—or, rather, her men—charged upon the outlaws. "Py chiminelli Got, I yoost gids oudt from deser places right avay off quick, py tam!"

Making immediate use of the first opportunity, he fled and made his way back toward the Mission.

He had gone but a mile or so in his flight when he met Jim Madison and Fred Wimmer—the latter an old chum of Jim's—on their way to join the outlaws, in order to aid them in plundering the city, which they supposed to be destroyed by that time.

"Hello there—you crazy Dutchman! What's up now?" demanded Jim, as the frightened Dutchman came panting down the road.

"Oop? Py chiminelli Got py toonder now! Effry pody ish oop! Effry pody ish kilt, py tam, but meer! Py Cheeses, dot Kids und dot chiants und, py chiminelli toonder, ein tousand more podies dey sharges mit us down de goolch, und dey kilts effry tamt von of us!"

"What does the crazy fool mean, Fred? Ask him in Dutch, and see what's up," cried Jim, now thoroughly excited.

In a few minutes Dutch John told of the tragedy at

the dam, the speedy fate of the outlaws and his escape—unconsciously telling the truth, for at that very moment the sound of fire-arms which had been borne to them on the wind ceased. Except Dutch John, every man who had taken part in the bloody work lay dead or was taken captive back to the town which they had sought to flood and pillage.

"Py Cheeses!" exclaimed the Dutchman. "Ve hafs to git oudt from deser country ride away off quicker as der tifle, or ve yoost vas a goner, py toonder!"

"That's right," said Jim. "We've got to get out of here mighty quick. Come on, boys! Let us pull out for San Francisco. We've got the funds that belonged to Faro Bill and his pard. We can whack up."

Three weeks later the trio of friends landed in San Francisco. Here, as well as at several other places, they saw the advertisement offering $1,000 for the arrest—or information that would lead to the arrest—of Jim Madison and Dutch John.

"Py chiminelli Got! Dose tifles are after us—yoost so sure as Got, py toonder!" said Dutch John.

For several weeks after arriving in the city they watched and waited in the hope of learning something of the whereabouts of Tom and the Kid, and to find out what they were up to; but, as yet, nothing definite could be learned.

"I have a plan," said Jim Madison, one day, after reading a new advertisement which raised the reward for his arrest from $1,000 to $2,000. "We must act at once, or, the very first thing that we know, some infernal detective will gather us in, along with that $2,000. My plan is this, and I think it will work, if we are only careful and don't get rattled at the last minute. We can rent a building and go into business. I have my eye on a place that will answer our purpose first-rate—a saloon down on Wharf street. It is a rather tough place, but that is just so much in its favor. The place is for rent, and we can have it remodeled to suit our wishes. When the trap is ready to spring, we can answer that advertisement with its shining bait of $2,000, and have our anxious moneyed friends come here. Then we must proceed in this fashion: Let Fred act as a private detective who has run us to cover. He can answer their advertisement and bring them here to meet him at his office. This office we can fit up in our building expressly for this purpose. Once we get him there, we three can manage him all right. A long, keen-bladed knife under the left ribs will settle him."

"Py chiminy Cheeses toonder! I toandt vants der chobs to do dot peesness, I petter peliefs meer! You haf to tickle his ribs mitoudt my helps, py toonder!" said the Dutchman, whose previous meetings with Tom Weston were vivid recollections.

"I can easily arrange that. Now, the first step is to get the saloon," said Jim.

This was the first step, and it was soon taken. The next day they rented and took possession of the place, which was said to be the most disreputable dive in the low district of San Francisco. Yet the house and its neighborhood suited their tastes and purposes.

In the course of a week, the details had been fixed for the execution of a plan which involved both abduction and murder.

A room had been fitted up in the back part of the building, on the second floor, and they had so laid their plan of action that they saw no chance for defeat.

Said Jim: "Let us see, now, if our plan will work all right. I take my place. John is the victim; Fred is the detective."

Entering the room which they had fitted up as the private office, they arranged the furniture as desired for carrying out their plan of murder.

On one side of the room a curtain was drawn—for the ostensible purpose of concealing a bed. A table was placed a few feet from the curtain and directly in front of the place where the curtain parted to serve the purpose of a door. Behind the table and directly between it and the parting in the curtain was a chair. Another chair was placed on the opposite side of the table from the first one, in front of which was a writing desk, upon which were writing materials.

When these things were arranged satisfactorily, Fred and Dutch John went out, and Jim took his place behind the curtain and awaited the reappearance of the other two. Presently the door opened and Fred and John entered. The supposed detective, leading the way, threw himself carelessly into the chair before the table, and at the same time motioned Dutch John to the chair behind the table. He then began conversation with reference to the arrest of Jim Madison.

At the proper time, the curtain parted and Jim Madison, knife in hand, stood directly behind the Dutchman and within easy reach of him.

"Py chiminy Cheeses! Dot vas petter as goot, py toonder! Dot takes him in all right—yoost so sure as tam! Py toonder, noddings vas petter!"

But Dutch John's hearty approval of the plan was owing to the fact that he was cast for a minor part in the tragedy.

Now that all was ready and each understood his part perfectly, the advertisement was answered, and they awaited impatiently the developments of their scheme.

But there was one thing yet—a last resort—which concerned Jim more than the others. There was a bare possibility that their scheme might not work just as they had planned; and so, to make sure of the girl, at least, a note was prepared as if written by Tom, directing her to come immediately in the carriage which would be sent for her, to meet Tom at a certain place, as he had made the arrest and wanted her to identify Jim.

Impatiently they awaited the arrival of Tom Weston and Edith, who were expected upon the evening train at ten o'clock.

As the train rolled into the depot, Tom and Edith stepped upon the platform and were immediately accosted by the supposed detective.

"Ah—yes," said Tom, as the detective introduced himself. "I am anxious to be through with this job as soon as possible. When I have seen this lady to a hotel, I will be at your service."

A hack was called, and in a few minutes drove them to the Golden Gate Hotel, where they registered and Tom saw that Edith was made comfortable. He then accompanied the bogus detective to his "private office."

"Come in, sir," said the detective, who was scarcely able to conceal his excitement. Entering the room, he motioned Tom to the chair behind the table, while he sat down in the other chair. Elevating his feet upon the corner of the table, he began to fumble among some papers, as if searching for a particular document. His hand trembled and his face turned pale—facts which Tom immediately noticed. Instantly a flash of suspicion crossed his mind, and, seeing the detective cast an anxious glance toward the curtain, he moved his chair a little and glanced hastily around.

What he saw might well have paralyzed a less courageous man. On Tom the sight had the opposite effect.

"PUTTING ON HER WRAPS QUICKLY."

Quick as a flash, Tom sprang aside, and the murderous knife which was aimed for his heart buried itself in the deal table.

Directly behind Jim Madison, who had struck the murderous blow, stood Dutch John armed with a double-barreled shotgun, which he was pointing, as nearly as his trembling hands would allow, directly at Tom's head.

With one bound Tom went out of the door, and, backing down stairs, he soon reached the street.

"Quick! Quick!" cried Jim. "Let 's go after the girl!"

Running down into a back alley, where a carriage was waiting, they sprang into it and drove to the hotel where Edith was stopping.

Ten minutes later they drove up to the hotel, and the detective entered and delivered to Edith his bogus message, adding: "We have got him!"

But Edith did not hear what the man was saying. Putting on her wraps as quickly as possible, she reported herself ready. A minute afterward, she entered the carriage with the detective.

Ten minutes later, Tom Weston entered the hotel and asked for Miss Edith, but she had gone—no one knew where. Some one had called for her, and she had gone away with him.

CHAPTER XXIV.

EDITH DRUGGED AND PLACED ON BOARD A VESSEL BOUND FOR AUSTRALIA.

After a mile of rapid driving, the carriage containing Edith and the detective stopped before a low, rough-looking boarding-house, which was kept by Dame Gaatsmann. Conditional arrangements had already been made, in case they should find it necessary to bring Edith there.

Here Edith was hurried from the carriage and into an upper room, in the back part of the house, overlooking a yard below, which was surrounded by a high board fence, completely shutting out all view of the building from the outside.

Her feelings, when she found herself a prisoner, can better be imagined than described. The awful truth at once forced itself upon her mind; and, with a pitiful moan, she sank down upon the bed. Burying her face in the pillow, she burst into a passionate fit of weeping.

Next morning Dame Gaatsmann brought Edith her breakfast, but she was deaf to the girl's entreaties, and when her work was done she went away and left the disheartened prisoner alone.

"O my God! What shall I do? Oh, if I had only remembered what Tom told me! But I did not know—I thought he had sent for me. O God, help me!"

Just then the door was opened, and she found herself face to face with her father's murderer—Jim Madison.

"STOP, JIM MADISON!"

"Ah, my beautiful little Edith!" cried Jim triumphantly. "And so I have got you at last, my darling! My beautiful little bird!"

Poor Edith! What could she do? What could she say? Her distress, her tears, her piteous entreaties—all were alike sweet music in the ears of her cowardly and heartless captor.

Words of love, threats and the most cruel insults were forced upon her unwilling ears. His base, low and dishonorable nature was shown in the shameless offers and promises to which he compelled her to listen. But, of course, these were without avail.

Scarlet with shame and quivering in every nerve from the intense hatred and anger which she could not control, she shrank away from the vile wretch and in a voice hoarse with resentment she commanded, as she turned her blazing eyes, black as midnight now in her rage, full upon the cowardly countenance of her abductor:

• "Stop! Not another word of insult, or, by the God to whom I look and pray for protection and strength, I will kill you like a dog—like the dog that you are! O my God! That a man whom I once looked upon as a friend—whom I believed to be honorable and true—ever should sink to this! I do not fear *you!* You need not think to conquer me by your base and cowardly threats! My father's *murderer!* Great God! Forgive me for the terrible feeling—the terrible desire for vengeance—that fills my heart! Oh, I could kill you, Jim Madison! I could kill you!"

These awful words rang like shrieks in the murderer's

ears. That dangerous light which flashed from her dark eyes sent a thrill of fear to the coward's heart, for well did he know the girl's masterly strength and indomitable courage.

Instinctively the cowering wretch shrank back until his hand rested upon the door knob.

Once the almost irresistable desire to kill her father's murderer and thus at once avenge his death and end her work nearly overcame her better nature. But with a shudder at what she thought to be a wicked passion, she controlled herself and allowed him to leave the room. However, the dangerous part of her nature, which had been nursed and encouraged by the rough, wild life that she had lived in the mines, and her insatiable desire for vengeance, as well as the irrevocable vow which she had made that day at the "burying," over the dead body of her mother, to avenge her father's murder and her good mother's death by grief thereat, had shown itself so unmistakably to Jim Madison that he never afterward dared to provoke her rage to such a degree.

For three days Edith was kept a close prisoner. At the end of the third day she ate supper and then lay down upon her bed and went to sleep.

How long she had slept, she knew not, when she was awakened by that peculiar feeling of uneasiness so often experienced when, for the first time, one finds himself on shipboard.

Arising from the couch on which she was lying, she found herself in a small room, and she knew from the heaving, rolling motion that she was at sea and aboard a small vessel.

What kind of a vessel it was and whither it might be bound were alike unanswerable questions to the captive. What could it mean and how came she there were questions not so hard to answer, for she comprehended her situation; she felt satisfied from the stupid, sleepy feeling which possessed her, that she had been given a drug before being conveyed from Dame Gaatsmann's prison to the vessel. Soon after awaking, the door of her room opened and her tormenter, Jim Madison, walked in.

"She Lay Down Without Undressing."

His handsome face showed surprise and disappointment at finding his supposed victim awake and recovered from the effects of the drug, which he had hired Dame Gaatsmann to administer by skillfully mixing it with the food which she brought to the prisoner.

With an ill-concealed attempt to hide his disappointment, Jim said: "Ah! I am happy to see you feeling and looking so well, Miss Edith."

"Indeed, sir? I had judged, from your appearance, that you were far from pleased. Please be seated, Mr. Madison," said Edith, with an imperious wave of her hand toward the only chair in the room. "I want to speak with you. I want to understand what is meant by this outrage. Stop!"

Fiercely her dark eyes flashed, and one little hand which had stolen beneath the folds of her dress returned grasping the butt of a jeweled revolver. She stepped between him and the door.

"Stop, Jim Madison, or so help me God you shall never leave this room alive! Oh, I could kill you! I could *kill* you!" She hissed these words in a voice so low and fierce that the cowering wretch sank into the chair in the most abject fear and trembling. "Tell me what vessel is this? Where are we going and how came I here?" And again her wild, fiercely flashing eyes were set on his, which were quickly averted.

But Jim Madison was speechless. How could this monster make answer?

"A thousand times death rather than suffer the disgrace, shame and misery that I would endure were I to revoke my vow of vengeance, as you ask me to do, and allow you to go unpunished! No! I will die first—and so shall you, Jim Madison. I will, so help me God—I *will* kill you, if ever you attempt to wrong me! Now tell me, sir, whose vessel is this?"

"It is mine."

"Whither bound?"

"To Australia."

"What do you mean, Jim Madison, by this most outrageous proceeding? Why have you brought me here?"

"Because I love you. O Edith——"

"Stop! Stop! I can 't—I won't—stand it! I will

kill you! Richly and many times over you deserve the murderer's fate."

"Don't, Edith! Remember that you are a woman—a lady."

"A woman—a lady!" cried the girl, bitterly. "A woman? Yes—I forgot. A lady? Oh, I fought once; and may God forgive me for the unwomanly act—if so it be—of taking human life! Yes—I fought then; and if need be, I can and will fight again."

Right well did Jim Madison know that Edith, under provocation involving danger, would keep her word.

He knew of the desperate ride that dark night, and the part that she had played in the bloody tragedy at the dam. He knew, from what he had seen of her at Las Animas, how fearless she really was; and he knew, too, that if forced to it she would fight with the relentless desperation of a tigress. He had tested her strength on the night that he, assisted by Faro Bill and One-Eyed Riley, had kidnaped her from the lonely tent. He was aware that, girl though she was, in a fair fight he would be no match for her. He realized now that he was at her mercy; and most heartily did he regret the step that he had taken. Still, he dared not release her; and to attempt her life was certainly to risk his own.

He could see one course only—strategy.

She had at least one weak point. So scrupulously honest and sincere herself, she could not understand the treachery and perfidy of her unscrupulous enemies; and for this reason she was too ready and willing to place confidence in their fair promises.

"Edith, there is no need of further war between us. I have made a mistake in what I have done; but if you knew—if you understood my motive——"

"If I knew—if I understood your motive? I pray God that I do not. A mistake? Yes—and a fatal one, too; for I have a friend who will avenge the wrongs and insults which you have heaped upon me. You can not escape Tom Weston. He is on your trail, and he will see that you pay the penalty for your crimes."

"But I will send you back, Edith. I will put you on the first vessel we meet that is bound for San Francisco. I swear it, Edith," pleaded the frightened villain.

"O sir! Will you do that?"

"Yes, I will—provided you will promise to let-up on me. Edith, will you give up——"

"Never! Go your way—do your worst! I fear you not! I will hear no more. Go!"

"Edith, you shall see the day when you will regret this step. I have offered you all that I possibly can. I have offered you freedom—conditioned only on my own freedom from your persecution. I can offer no more. You are my prisoner, you are in my power; and it is for my own protection that I have taken this step. If you will not accept my terms, then I must——"

"Spare your threats! It is not only unmanly in you to threaten a girl, but it is useless as well; for I do not fear you. I can accept no terms from my father's murderer. Ours is a war to the death. Go, now; I will not hear you."

He went, and was glad of the opportunity to escape

"She Dropped Lightly into the Water."
---198---

from Edith's presence. After this last violent outburst of passion, Jim realized that he stood on very daugerous ground.

The foiled villain could only mutter: "If I had only known that she was armed, and had taken the precaution to disarm her! But, then, I did n't expect her to recover so soon."

CHAPTER XXV.

EDITH ONCE MORE DONS BOY HABILIMENTS AND IN THE DEAD OF NIGHT LEAPS INTO THE SEA.

Day after day passed, and the vessel kept steadily on her course.

Shut up as she was in her little prison room, the poor girl passed the weary days alone; for she would not permit Jim Madison to enter the door. She would allow no one except Dutch John to wait on her. In due time the vessel reached the shores of Australia, and came to anchor near a small town on the eastern coast.

Again Madison endeavored to bring the brave girl to terms, but she would not permit him to enter her room, nor would she listen to his entreaties.

For several days they remained near the town, but the prisoner was not permitted to leave her room.

After replenishing their store of provisions, they again set sail and coasted along the shore for several days, when they finally came to anchor near Sidney. Here, from a conversation which she had overheard, Edith learned that Tom had pursued them to Australia, and was even then hot on their trail. She gleaned from the excited words and manner of her captors that they were sorely distressed at the close and persistent pursuit, and were fearful lest they should be discovered before they could make their escape from the harbor. But the harbor was cleared without detection, and the flight was renewed.

"Py chiminy!" exclaimed Dutch John, as the boat sailed out of the harbor. "Dot ish pad peesness, py chiminelli toonder! I yoost gids right oudt from deser ships quick, right avay off, py tam!"

COASTING ALONG THE SHORE.

"What 's up now, Dutchy?" asked Jim, as he heard the Dutchman's discontented muttering.

"Vat 's oop? Py Cheeses toonder! Der tifle est oop! Py tam, I leafs deser ships right avay off alretty! Dot tifle of a chiant—dot Tom Veston—ish here alretty pefore ve here comes, und, py Got in himmel, he catches us right avay off!"

"But if you leave the vessel and go ashore, he will be sure to catch you. He will set the whole police force after us," said Jim.

"Ve gifs oop dot girls, und den he leafs us alone, py tam!" cried the Dutchman, excitedly.

"But he won't do any thing of the kind," declared Jim. "Our only chance of escape is to put him out of the way, and we must do it."

"Py toonder, you shall put him oudt of de vay alretty. I hafs noddings to do mit dot peesness. I sees dot girls, und I talks mit him apoudt dot peesness, py toonder!" said the Dutchman.

"You can't do any thing with her," declared Jim. "You shall not see her. She is my prisoner—my property. You shall not interfere with my plans." Stepping between John and the cabin door, Jim barred the way.

"Py toonder, I leafs deser ships right avay off quick, und you goes mit ter tifle, py chiminy!"

Dutch John made his threat good. Later in the day, on coming in sight of a small town, he demanded to be put off.

"I don't like this, Jim," said Fred, as the Dutchman was put ashore.

"Neither do I," replied Jim. "We ought never to have let him go."

"We had better put the girl ashore than Dutchy," said Fred.

"But I tell you, Fred, it won't make any difference. That infernal Weston will never stop until he gets a bullet through his heart. We've got to do him!" said Jim.

"And the girl is just as dangerous as he is," declared Fred. "You are afraid of her, and you can't do anything with her. Then why not put her ashore?"

"I tell you, Fred, that won't do. She is just as much to be feared as he."

"Then put her out of the way, too," suggested Fred.

Bad man though he was, Jim Madison recoiled with terror at the bare mention of such a deed.

He remembered her when a beautiful girl at home, and now that she had grown to be a woman, in his eyes she was more beautiful than ever. Though he feared her when her temper was aroused, he loved her madly.

"No—no," he exclaimed. "She shall yet be mine. I have a plan. All I want now is to get Tom Weston out of the way."

"And do you think that the girl will marry you—her father's murderer?" asked Fred, contemptuously.

"No. But what do I care whether she will marry me or not? Bah! I don't want to marry her."

To the impatient and uneasy Fred he then unfolded in detail his shameless plot to break Edith's proud spirit and crush her heart.

The evening was fast drawing to a close, and the night gave promise of being dark and stormy. Dark clouds were already beginning to loom up in the west, and vivid flashes of forked lightning darted out behind the fringed edges of a bank of inky-black clouds just rising above the water-bound horizon. Muttering thunder came rolling over the still water.

The sails hung lifeless; not a breath of air stirred, and

that dread stillness—that dread calm which so often precedes the coming tempest—had caught the vessel while it was yet a mile from the nearest sheltered cove.

Edith was sitting by the only window in her room—a small window, apparently not more than a foot wide by a foot and a half in length—and hung upon hinges so it could be opened easily. She sat there, looking dreamily out over the dark-green sea and wondering what all the bustle and stir which was going on above could mean, when she heard the captain giving orders to get out the boats and tow the vessel to the shore.

Her room in the cabin, situated as it was back in the stern of the vessel, hid the boats and men from view, so that she could not see their movements, and in consequence her own movements could not be seen by the men.

"Ah," she mused, "now is my time!"

Listening to assure herself that no one was on deck, she began removing her garments. In a minute or two she stood arrayed in a suit of boy's clothes, which she had stealthily and skillfully made from her under clothing.

Then, opening the small window, she squeezed herself through and dropped lightly into the water below.

—:o:—

CHAPTER XXVI.

THE FURY OF THE TEMPEST BREAKS OVER THE HEAD OF THE WAVE-TOSSED WAIF.

Darkness had already closed down over the sea, and Edith, as she dropped into the dark, cold water, struck boldly out, as nearly as she could determine, toward the shore. In a few minutes the vessel, which was the only visible thing about her, had disappeared in the darkness which enveloped the face of the deep.

Oh, how lonely did the poor, homeless girl feel as she found herself alone in the dark, cold water and saw the inky blackness of night closing about her! She could see nothing save the vivid flash of the red tongues of flame which leaped from the huge columns of cloud that came marching silently and swiftly over the surface of the yet placid sea.

On—swiftly on—came the silent storm. For a brief spell the low, ominous mutterings had ceased, as if the tempest were gathering new strength and fury for the awful work of devastation and ruin before it.

On swept the dark column—towering high above her now, then reaching out its giant arms like the wings of a great net, extending far beyond her on either side and circling around as if to clasp her in a deadly embrace.

Then burst forth the vivid tongues of flame, which darted down into the now troubled waters. The storm, hanging for a moment as if gloating over its helpless vic-

"Look Look"!! Cried the Old Sea Captain.

'tim, came rushing down like a host of demons let loose for destruction.

Not for a moment did the brave girl despair. As soon as the prison ship was out of sight, she had made for the shore. Slim hope, indeed, there seemed to be for the dauntless girl. A mile of water between herself and the land—a fiercely raging tempest rushing down on her, tossing the sea into foaming, mountainous billows in its mad fury as it came! What hope?

"She Struck Boldly for the Shore."

"O God! Must I die? Oh, that I could live to fulfill my vow—to avenge my good father's cruel murder! Let me live, O God! Let me live, for life is so sweet to me now! O Tom! That I should be taken from you now, and not be spared to reward your noble heart for the love you gave me!"

This was the silent prayer of Edith's filial soul—the appeal of her loyal heart.

Just then a bright flash of light gleamed across the dark waters. With a great bound, her heart—for so it seemed—leaped into her throat, and for a moment smothered the glad cry which strove for utterance. But this hindered for a moment only. Then burst forth the joyous cry, ringing loud and clear above the roar of the rushing tempest:

"Help! Help!"

Quickly and with a tremor of terror came the fearful thought: What if they should prove to be Jim Madison and his men searching for her?

"Oh, if they should be Jim and his men! No—no! They shall not take me. They are coming—oh, they are coming!"

She saw the light, which was a ship's lantern, held in the hand of a man standing in the bow of a life boat, flash across the water. Again she cried:

"Help! Help!"

"Pull hard!" commanded the man in the bow of the approaching boat, as he leaned eagerly forward and tried to peer into the darkness.

"Pull—you lubbers!" thundered the old sea captain, rising and scanning the surface of the sea.

"O God!" cried the man with the lantern, as the storm burst upon them like a legion of furies. "Too late! Too late!"

"Look! Look!" cried the old sea captain, pointing his finger to where the black line of water was lashed into foam by the tempest.

One bound, and the life boat was at the spot.

"Stern all!" thundered the old sea captain. A little white object was seen almost beneath the bow of the boat, and two white arms were raised imploringly.

The lantern dropped, and the man in the bow of the

"HOLD HER FAST!"

boat, bending low, seized the now almost exhausted girl in his strong hands. In another moment he clasped the drenched and shivering form to his heart.

CHAPTER XXVII.

THE OLD SEA CAPTAIN GIVES ORDERS TO HIS CREW—
TOM WESTON OBEYS THEM.

"Edith!" whispered the man, and his feverish lips pressed her own.

"Tom!"

A golden head, with the salt-sea brine sparkling among shining curls, drooped upon his broad, manly bosom and the delicate form, shivering with cold, nestled close to the heart which loved and protected.

"Lay to your oars!" commanded the captain, "and pull for the shore."

With swift strokes the men sent the life boat humming through the raging waters.

"Blast my old head lights!" exclaimed the old sea captain, rubbing the salt spray from his eyes and taking another look at beautiful Edith. "Stove my bulkhead, now!"

"Here, Kid," said Tom, removing his coat and wrapping it about her. "There—that will keep you warm some. Now, sit close to me, so as to keep warm. You are quite chilled, my darling."

"Thank you, Tom," murmured the girl, as she crouched, cold and shivering, close to his side, while his strong right arm stole gently about her lithe form, and drew her close to him.

Crouching low in the bow of the boat, in order to shelter themselves from the icy spray which, driven by the wintry Australian wind, froze upon their clothing, Tom strove to shield and revive his fiancée.

"Are you warmer now, Kid?"

"Yes. I am getting warm now, Tom. And I see that you do not use your arm yet. How is your shoulder, Tom?"

"It is no worse—perhaps a little better. But my little girl—how is she?"

"Oh, I am nearly well—just a little sore and lame."

"My poor, wounded dove!"

"Tom!"

"No—no! I won't do it again, Kid. But O my darling—I mean Kid—how could you do such a thing? You surely would have been drowned but for these brave fellows. Tell me, my—Kid—how did it happen?"

"Here," interrupted the gruff old sea captain, who took off his great coat and threw it over Edith's head and shoulders. "Poor child!"

"Tell me now," whispered Tom, with his lips so near her cheek that no wonder the subtle influence—attraction, gravitation, love or what you may—proved too strong for him. For Tom had his weak points, and when he looked down into those beautiful eyes—so wide and so full of love—and then those lips, so temptingly close —there is no wonder   Just a faint remonstrative struggle on her part—but the great coat hid them from view, the tempest roared and hissed, the men bent to their oars and the old sea captain, in his deep bass, thundered:

"Hold her to it!"

"Tom!" remonstrated Edith.

"But the captain said so, and we have to obey orders," declared Tom, and he drew her still closer.

"Tom!"

"I won't do it again, Kid. Now, tell me how it all happened."

"Oh, I made up my mind that I would leave the vessel the first opportunity that I got. I had been preparing for it for several days, but they kept such a close watch that I have had no opportunity until to-night. All that bothered me was my clothes. I could n't swim with my dresses on, so I had to make me a suit of boy's things; but I nearly failed for lack of material. Tonight, when they saw the storm coming up, as there was no wind, they got out the boats, and with long ropes began towing the ship toward the shore. They were all in the boats, I think, for I could n't hear any one on deck, and

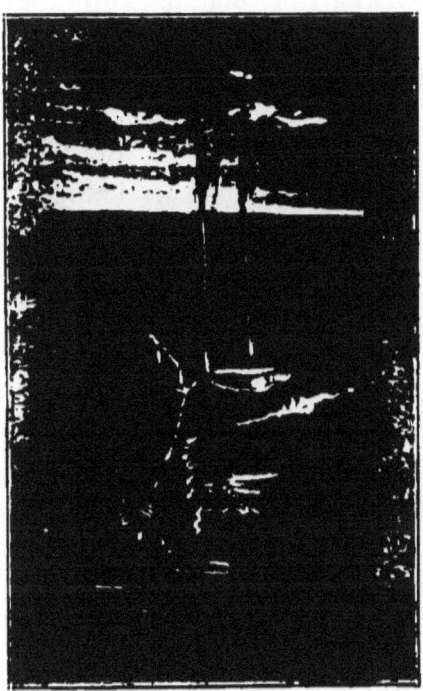

Towing the Vessel to Shore.

I knew that my opportunity had come. So I crawled out of the little window of my cabin, and dropped into the water. O Tom, I was not certain that I could swim to the shore, but I could n't help it. I had to leave the vessel tonight, Tom. O God! It makes me sick when I think of what I heard Jim and Fred planning after they put Dutch John ashore."

"Put Dutch John ashore? What did they do that for, Kid? When did they put him ashore?"

"It was about four o'clock this afternoon; but I can not say what they did it for. The two quarreled about some thing, but I could not hear what the matter was."

"Why did you have to leave the vessel, Kid? What was it that you overheard them saying?"

"O Tom! I can not tell you now. Perhaps, some time, I can."

Involuntarily Tom's eyes flashed fire and his fists clinched. "I can well imagine the purport of their confab. The infernal——"

"Tom!" cried Edith, reproachfully. "Please do not swear."

"I can't help it, Kid; it makes me boil. Oh, they shall suffer for this."

"Say, Tom! How did you happen to be here just in time to save me?"

"You may be sure I did not 'happen' to be here; it was no accident. We got here by the hardest kind of work. The united strength of twelve brave, strong men put me here."

"But how did it all happen?" persisted the brave girl.

"Oh, I was following the vessel, of course. I saw Dutch John in Sidney, just as he was pulling out for his vessel, and I rustled a boat and crew and set out in pursuit. We had followed as best we could, and were coming along the shore, when we came in sight of them—just as they began towing their vessel toward the shore. I was watching their movements. I had just told the captain that we would wait till they had nearly reached the shore, in order that we might the more easily pounce upon them, when I saw you crawl out of the window and drop into the water."

"How could you tell that it was I, Tom? You must have been two miles away."

"Oh, I have a good glass, of course. I purchased it at Sidney. Without the glass, I would never have seen you at all. It was the merest chance that I did see you, anyway, Kid. If you had been a moment sooner or a moment later, my darling little girl would have been at the bottom of the sea now."

As he said this, Tom pressed the shuddering Edith still closer to his heart, as if fearful that the sea might yet claim her.

"O Tom!"

A shudder passed over Edith at the remembrance of her awful danger and the miraculous rescue from her combined enemies—her abductors and the tempest.

"I can't help it, Tom—perhaps it is wrong for me to feel so—but God has given me back to you, and I love you with all my heart. Though I vowed not to seek pleasure or happiness till I had finished my work—had avenged the death of my father and mother—I can not help it, Tom, that you make me happy."

"It would be a far greater wrong for you, Kid, if you refused my love and the little pleasure and happiness which it brings to you; for it may lighten that burden of sorrow which has so nearly crushed your heart. No—no, Kid; don't do that. It comes not of your own seeking; rather, it is forced upon you. Accept it, then, for it can't be wrong."

"Tom, I do not refuse your love—so noble and true—for I love you with all my heart. Accept it, Tom, for I love you; and it is all that I have to give. But please wait until our work is done, Tom, and then———"

"And then?" echoed Tom.

"Oh, you need not ask, Tom; there is no need of that. Answer for me, Tom. Will this be satisfactory?"

"Satisfactory to me, darling."

"And to me, Tom."

And then—well, who can ever know? The great coat hid them from view; the wind roared and the tempest raged; the boat touched the shore and six brave men sprang out and seized the gunwales, and the old sea captain thundered:

"Hold her fast!"

This time the sweet, red lips did not shrink; instead there was a low whisper:

"Obey orders, Tom."

"Just the Fit, I Do Declare!"
---218---

CHAPTER XXVIII.

THE TWO INDOMITABLE AVENGERS ENJOY A BIT OF OLD-FASHIONED HOSPITALITY.

"Hold her fast!" shouted the old sea captain, and the six men clung to the gunwales. The others sprang out, seized the hawser and dragged the boat high above the reach of the angry waves.

"Come," said Tom. Supporting his rescued companion upon his arm and wrapping the captain's great coat snugly about her supple form, completely concealing her from view, he led her up the beach to a house but a short distance away.

"Come up with me to the house," said a hearty old tar. "My old woman will take care of the gal. Welcome, little waif."

And right welcome was she made to feel, too, when she reached the sailor's humble home.

"Come in!" exclaimed the kind, motherly old dame, seizing the shivering girl in her arms and half carrying her to the fire which blazed and crackled in the broad fire-place. "Poor child! You are chilled nearly through. There—there, my little deary! Now you'll get warm! Now you'll get warm!" As she said this, she placed Edith in the great arm chair. "There—there! Now a hot supper and then a warm bed will put new life into you."

Brisk as a girl, the old lady flew about from the fire to the table and from the table to the cupboard until, in an incredibly short time, a steaming supper was ready for her hungry guests.

"Sit up—sit up!" said the hospitable old dame, "and right welcome are ye. Let me help you, poor child!"

She swung Edith around to the table, poured out the fragrant coffee and bade her guests refresh themselves.

When supper was over, Edith was taken by the motherly lady to her own bed, and was soon snugly stowed away for the night. The men found warm and fairly comfortable berths in the large room near the fire.

"Oh, this is so warm and so nice!" thought the weary girl, as she found herself snugly tucked up in the bed.

THE OLD SEA CAPTAIN.

"Poor child!" said the old lady, as she stooped and kissed Edith's pale cheek.

Bright and early the next morning, the men were astir and preparing to renew the pursuit of the fugitives.

While breakfast was being prepared, Tom walked to

the village, a short distance away, and when he returned he brought with him a full suit of boy's clothes. These were to replace the improvised bathing suit in which his partner escaped from the ship.

"My good woman, please take these to the girl," said Tom.

"La, me!" exclaimed the old lady, as she spread the garments out for the girl's inspection. "Such nice woolen clothes, and just the fit, I do declare! And so soft, and warm, and fine, and fit for a prince!"

"Ah, Kid!" exclaimed Tom, as she entered the room. "You are looking better this morning than I expected to see you. How do you feel?"

"Quite well, I thank you, Tom. How do you feel after your last night's wetting?"

"Oh, I am all right," replied Tom.

"But your shoulder pains you, Tom; you look pale," said Edith, as she readjusted the sling which supported his crippled arm.

"Oh, that's nothing," said Tom, carelessly. "But come, Kid; breakfast is ready. We must eat and be off."

"Just so, Tom; there is no rest for us till our work is finished."

—:o:—

CHAPTER XXIX.

DUTCH JOHN RETURNS TO ARIZONA AND GIVES A LARGELY ATTENDED FAREWELL PERFORMANCE.

Breakfast was soon over, and then the boat was manned and again took up the search. Going along the shore, they entered the cove where, the night before, the vessel owned by Jim Madison and Fred Wimmer had sought refuge, and were greatly surprised at seeing a large crowd of people gathered about the wreck of a vessel lying upon a rocky point just inside the little cove.

"Look! Look!" cried Edith, pointing toward the wreck. "It's Jim Madison's vessel!"

A few more powerful strokes of the oars brought the searchers to the wreck. Just as they touched upon the beach, a man was seen to turn and walk rapidly away, as if anxious to escape the notice of the new-comers.

"Stop him! Stop that man!" cried Edith, pointing to the retreating form. "He is Dutch John!"

At the sound of this command the man broke into a run, but in a moment Tom Weston was upon him. Seizing him by the shoulder, Tom easily hurled him to the ground.

"O mein Got! Mein Got!" wailed the trembling Dutchman. "I'm kilt! I'm kilt, py Cheeses toonder! Kid! Kid!" he wailed, appealing to the tender-hearted girl. "Helpen meer, Kid! Py chiminy Got, I helpen ier—py tam I didt—und dot ish vy dey pounced meer right avay off alretty, py Cheeses!"

"HE HURLED HIM TO THE GROUND."

"No one shall hurt you, John," said the girl, pitying him in his wretched fear, in spite of the horrible part which he had played.

"Got pless ier, Kid! Got pless ier!" said John.

"Where is Madison? Speak, Dutchman—where is he?" demanded Tom.

"Py chiminelli Got, I toandt know. I toandt, py Cheeses! I yoost shwares, py chiminelli tam!"

"John was not on the vessel at the time of the wreck, Tom," interceded Edith. "I do not think he knows where Jim is now. They quarreled, and I think that it was something about me."

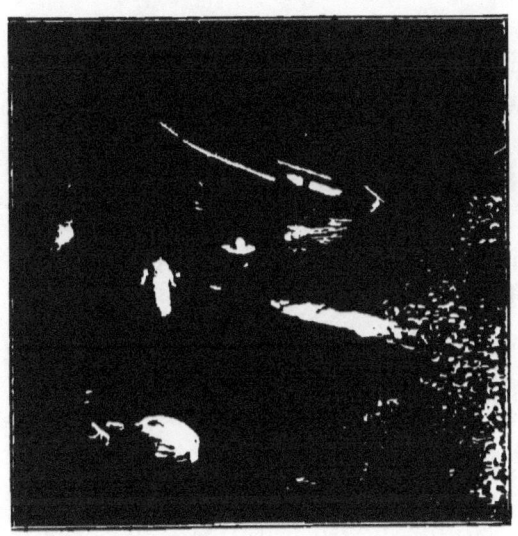

"A Crowd Gathered About the Wreck."

"Yah! Yah, mein Herr Tom; I shwares, py tam, dot it yoost vas apoudt dot Kids, so helpen me Got, py Cheeses! I yoost would n't let 'em kilts dot Kids; und, py tam, dey puts meer right avay off quick ashore, py Cheeses!"

The wreck was searched, and four bodies were found; but neither Madison nor Wimmer was among them.

"Well, Kid," said Tom, when they had returned from a long and fruitless search, "our work is not yet finished. Come; let us be about."

"What shall we do with Dutch John?" asked Edith.

"Oh, these men will take care of him all right," said Tom. "You know, there is a reward of $1,000 for his arrest."

"Oh, py chiminy toonder, I gifs ier ten tousand tollar if ze leefs meer go, py chiminelli Got, right avay off quick, py tam!" cried the Dutchman in despair.

But his offers were made to deaf ears, for he was immediately taken to Sidney and turned over to the authorities. Not long afterward he was returned to the town of Ruby Gulch, to answer to the charge preferred against him there of participating in the attempt to break the dam and destroy the town.

In the mining districts of Arizona, as we have heretofore had occasion to see, justice is swift; and in this case it did not break its long established precedent.

Dutch John stood for one awful moment upon the scaffold and looked down on the sea of faces about him, but his tongue clove to his mouth with fear, and he was mute.

Wild and long rang the shouts of triumph as the trap fell, and Dutch John swung suspended by his neck. His body was then riddled with a thousand bullets from the guns and revolvers of the excited mob.

"EDITH EMERGED FROM THE DRESS MAKER'S ESTABLISHMENT."

CHAPTER XXX.

THE CAPTAIN OF A MERCHANTMAN IS CONFRONTED BY A PUZZLE, WHICH TOM AND EDITH SOLVE.

Three days passed before any trace of the fugitives could be found, and five days later they were traced to Sidney.

For several days no further trace of them could be found; but finally Tom and the Kid became satisfied, from what they were able to learn, that the fugitives had embarked for New York.

"Nothing remains, Edith, but for us to follow them," declared Tom. "It will be a long chase, and Jim will have a great advantage of us if he gets there; for he is acquainted in New York and has lots of friends and old cronies there who are, no doubt, just as bad as he is. New York is full of such people, and if one is acquainted with them and knows where to find them he has a great advantage over a stranger, especially if the stranger is an enemy to that class of people."

"Of course, we must follow them, Tom," declared the dauntless girl. "The trip will give us time to rest up a little, and will give your shoulder a chance to get well. But I must have some clothes, Tom. I can't disguise myself as a boy any longer; beside, I do not think it is necessary. I can get ready-made clothing here, I think, without trouble."

"Well, suit yourself," said Tom. "You can go and

get what you want while I am looking up a ship that is bound for America."

"No. I want you to go with me," said Edith. "Then I will go with you. I may be foolish, Tom, but I can't help it; so come along. It will take but a little while. We will go to a dress maker's first, and then go down to the harbor."

"Well, come on then," said Tom, and in a few hours Edith emerged from the dress maker's establishment and greeted her waiting companion a full fledged and remarkably handsome young lady.

"Oh, I feel so much better now!" exclaimed Edith. "I feel like myself again. Now I am ready to resume work; so lead the way, Tom."

"We will go down among the shipping houses and see about getting passage to New York, and when we can go. I have already telegraphed the police, and I have raised the reward for Jim's arrest to $10,000," said Tom, as they wended their way down toward the docks.

Here they learned that there would be no regular steamship for America short of a week; so it would be impossible for them to go before that time, unless by some other way.

"We can not wait that long, Tom," declared Edith. "Let us go by some other way, if we can."

"If you had been here yesterday," said an old sailor, "you could have gone on board the Australian. There were two young fellows here hunting for a passage, and I told them of her, and they went."

"What for looking fellows were they?" asked Tom.

"They were the same as you described," replied the man.

"There is a merchantman here loading for New York that starts today. You can go on her, I think, if you

"If You Had Been Here Yesterday," Said an Old Sailor.

prefer to go that way," said a shipping agent. "I will look the matter up for you, if you want me to."

"I thank you. We will be very glad to have you do so, for our business is urgent. When may I expect to be taken aboard?" asked Tom.

"She sails in about two hours. Ah, here comes the captain now. Captain Westermann, a lady and gentleman looking for a passage to New York. I was just speaking to them of you."

"Captain Westermann, I am happy to meet you just at this particular time, as I am very anxious to get to New York as soon as possible. My business is important and time is precious," said Tom, earnestly.

Captain Westermann stroked his long beard, and for a few moments looked at the ground thoughtfully.

"I have two passengers now for whom I had to make room, just to accommodate them, as they were anxious to reach New York on pressing business. I was full before I took them in, and I could not possibly make room for more than one. I have no accommodations for a lady."

"I can put up with any thing. Only say that I can go," pleaded Edith.

"I would be glad to accommodate you, but——."

"Say that we can go!" pleaded the beautiful girl, earnestly, beseechingly, her dark eyes filling with tears as she looked up into the bronzed face of the captain with such a pitiful glance that it went to the captain's heart. Beautiful little Edith could be well nigh irresistable when she had a mind to be, and she exerted her utmost power of enchantment now.

"My dear little lady," remonstrated the captain, almost at his wits' end. "I could not possibly provide for you. There is not a single berth in the ship, except one in my state room. If you were a man, or even if you were this man's wife—"beg pardon, my dear lady," said the captain hastily, as he saw a deep blush crimson the fair cheek of the girl—"it would, indeed, make all the difference in the world."

"How long before you will start?" asked Tom.

"In two hours. But I could delay an hour or two, if it were absolutely necessary," replied the captain.

"What shall we do, Kid?" asked Tom, taking her to one side.

"O Tom! I don't know," replied the girl, with downcast eyes and blushing cheeks. "What do you say, Tom? What shall we do?"

"We can do one of two things, Kid. We can get married and go with him, or we can remain here and wait for another vessel."

"But what shall we do, Tom? Tell me," pleaded the girl.

"No—no; I won't do that, Kid. You must decide for yourself."

"But you will advise me, Tom. Please tell me what you think," pleaded the girl, earnestly. "Pity me, Tom, for I am but a poor, weak, little girl, with no one to go to with my troubles but you. Do tell me; I will do whatever you advise."

"I can not take advantage of you, Kid; it is no use; I can not do it."

"But you will not, Tom; I know you will not take advantage of me because of this."

"Well, we will wait," said Tom, and he turned away.

"Tom, don't let your love for me interfere with our work. I am too young, I know. I—I am afraid that you would be disappointed in me. As a girl, perhaps, I am all well enough; but as a wife, Tom, I am afraid I would be a failure."

"Nonsense, Kid! Seventeen is quite old enough. But are you quite sure that you are willing to do this?"

"I will do any thing to accomplish my work. And I do not fear, Tom, that I will ever have cause to regret the step."

"Then may God help me if I do you wrong, Edith. Come; let us go and be married."

"Well," said the captain, who had been waiting, for his heart told him what the conference was about, "is there any new arrangement? I am very loath to disappoint you."

"We will be married," replied Tom.

"Very well. I will delay our starting till morning. Be here at six o'clock, and I will send a boat to fetch you off," said the captain.

"We thank you," replied Tom.

Next morning dawned bright and beautiful, and the glad sun shone down upon the fair and happy young bride with its warm, greeting rays, welcoming her to a new and happy life.

"O Tom!" exclaimed the happy bride, as the two—now one—strolled down the path and came out upon the sandy beach just where the long swell of the ocean came in and, climbing up over the bright, shining pebbles, broke in a long line of sparkling, silvery spray, and with a low, soft murmur whispered a welcome greeting to the happy little wife. "O Tom! I am so happy! It seems almost a sin—almost as though I had forgotten my vow to seek no happiness or pleasure till I had solved the mystery of my father's death and avenged the death of my poor, broken-hearted mother. Do you think that it is wrong, Tom?"

"No—no, Kid. It can not be wrong. So do not worry about that any more. You did not seek this—it has been forced upon you—my brave little girl. Perhaps such a generous, self-sacrificing heart as is yours deserves a better reward than the perils, sufferings and disappointments which have been your lot for the past two years. If it is the will of God that you should partake of a little pleasure now, after all these months and years of the bitterest woe, the most imminent peril and the most disheartening disappointments, be you content, my sweet little wife."

"O Tom—my brave, noble-hearted boy—I thank you with all my poor heart for your generous, reassuring words!"

Brave, gentle, noble-hearted Edith! Little did she dream now of the impending storms of misery and woe which were already hovering over her, as she stood upon the mountain heights of love and looked away even to the gates of that Celestial City within whose pale does supreme and eternal happiness reign—as she drank from that fount of sweet, joyous love flowing from the heart of a noble man, whose boundless love, pervading her soul, enrapturing her heart, cast a halo of glory about her.

Brave, noble, dauntless Edith! Happy bride of but a few short hours, whose young heart still throbbed with the first rapturous, crowning glory of a pure and lofty love—so soon to be made to drink to the dregs a bitter cup of woe, made still more bitter because of the sweets of love which she had so lately enjoyed.

CHAPTER XXXI.

THE BRIDE OF A DAY LEFT ALONE—TOM'S ABSENCE PROLONGED AND INEXPLICABLE.

"Ah, Tom!" exclaimed Edith as she glanced at a beautiful little watch that Tom had given her the night before. "It is just six o'clock, and the captain will be looking for us."

"Well, we must go, then," declared Tom. And in a few minutes they joined the captain on the dock.

"I wish you joy, my little lady!" exclaimed the captain, as he shook each heartily by the hand. "And now let us be off."

Entering the captain's boat, they were rowed to the ship—the City of Brooklyn—upon whose polished deck they soon found themselves.

"Pipe all hands to quarters!" commanded the captain. "We will sail immediately."

"Captain," said the mate, appearing before his superior. "Our two passengers are not aboard. They went ashore last night, and have not yet returned."

"How is this?" demanded the captain. "They were most anxious to be off. Send a boat ashore for them,

"She Found a Carriage Awaiting Her."

and if they are not found by ten o'clock we must sail and leave them."

"Aye—aye, sir!" responded the mate, and immediately gave the necessary orders.

"Who are these men, captain?" asked Tom.

"Mr. James and Mr. Brooks are the names," replied the captain.

"What for looking men are they?"

"One is a rather small fellow, slim, and one would call him handsome."

"Black eyes and a scar over the right one?" interrupted Tom.

"Yes—now that I think of it—he did have a scar over the right eye."

"By the eternal!" cried Tom, with suppressed excitement. "He is Jim Madison!"

"Jim Madison? What? The man for whom that $10,000 reward is offered?" gasped the captain.

"The same man, captain," replied Tom. "Hail the boat and let me go ashore with them. Stay here, Edith. The captain will show you to your room, and you can be arranging your things while I am gone. There—there! Do not look so scared. You will be as safe here as if you were at home. I will be back in a few hours, at the farthest. There," he said, as the captain showed them to their state room, "be a brave little girl." He kissed her good-by, and entered the boat.

Ten o'clock came, and the boat and its crew returned to the waiting ship; but neither Tom nor either of the missing passengers returned with the boat.

White and trembling, Edith stood awaiting in breathless silence an explanation.

"O sir!" she cried, as the mate sprang upon deck. "Where is Tom? What has happened?"

"Be calm, my lady. Nothing has happened—nothing at all. Here is a letter which the good man has sent to you," said the mate of the waiting City of Brooklyn, to whom Tom had intrusted the letter to his wife.

Eagerly she seized the message and ran to her room to read it. Hastily tearing open the envelope, she read as follows:

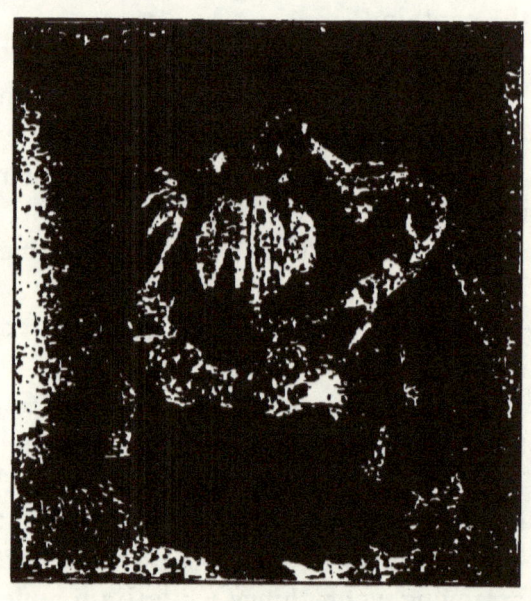

"Tearing Open the Envelope, She Read."

"My Sweet Little Wife: Do not be alarmed. I am all right, and have struck the trail of our victim. I can not come back for you, so have the captain put you ashore. I will send a carriage for you. Pay the captain for his trouble, and come as s on as possible to the Victoria Hotel, where we stayed last night. Stay there until I come. If I am not back before night, I will write and let you know all about it. Do not worry, Kid. From your own loving Tom."

With tearful eyes and a sad heart, the devoted young

wife obeyed the directions, and was soon put ashore. She found the carriage awaiting her and was driven to the Victoria Hotel, where she was shown to her bridal chamber of the night before.

Evening came at last, but no Tom.

"Oh, what can it mean?" moaned the half-distracted wife.

Just then a servant knocked and announced a letter for her. But it brought little comfort.

Uneasy, disappointed and sick at heart, Edith lay down on her bridal couch, and vainly sought sleep.

Days, weeks and months passed. Still Tom did not come.

However, Edith was not idle. Crushed though her heart was and well nigh despairing, she sought by every means in her power to find a clew that would guide her in discovering her husband's fate.

Heavily time dragged slowly on, and the long Winter months had passed. With the coming of Spring came the birds and the flowers, but no news of Tom came to cheer the weary heart of Edith. Sad and with aching heart, she could find no peace—no rest. All was dark and dreary. Many kind and sympathizing friends offered their consolation, and many were the conjectures made as to the probable fate of the missing man. It had even been hinted, and there were not wanting those ready to declare—and perhaps, too, with a color of probability—that the husband had deserted the poor girl. But Edith's ears were deaf to all disparaging theories.

"Oh, I can not stand this any longer!" cried the poor

girl, in very desperation, while some of her friends were offering their sympathy. In spite of the remonstrances of well meaning friends, the brave girl began the search.

Edith at once raised the reward for the apprehension of Jim Madison to $20,000. She also sent a description of Tom Weston to the leading newspapers of Australia, Europe and America, offering a reward for any information locating him.

CHAPTER XXXII.

CLEVER JIM MADISON ACCOMPLISHES THE DEATH OF TUCSON JOE AND THE CAPTURE OF TOM WESTON.

The evening that Edith and Tom Weston were married, as we have already seen, Jim Madison and Fred Wimmer—the Mr. James and Mr. Brooks who engaged passage on the merchantman City of Brooklyn—left the ship and did not return. Why they did so is thus accounted for: When the captain returned to the ship and countermanded his order to sail that day, he told the passengers the cause of the delay.

Jim's suspicions were immediately aroused, and so, to assure themselves that all was right, he and Fred went ashore and proceeded at once to the hotel where the wedding was to take place. As a result of this, they saw and recognized Weston, but they did not see Edith.

"Fred," said Jim, "we have got to do some thing. I would rather have the devil after me than that man. I tell you what it is: We have got to put that man out of the way, or our name is Dennis."

"Hello there—Tucson Joe! Whereaway?"

"But, if he sails for New York today—or, rather, in the morning—we will be rid of him, for a while at least, and it will give us a chance to get out of the way," suggested Fred.

"It will only give us a little time—that is all. He will surely follow us up. But who are these passengers for whom the captain is waiting? Weston can not well be one of them, for the captain said they were a gentleman and a lady, and were to be married tonight, in order to meet the proprieties of double-berth accommodations. Hence the captain's delay in sailing."

"At any rate, the lady in question can not be Edith; for, unless she bears a charmed life, she is dead. No swimmer that ever split water could have weathered the storm which raged that night," declared Fred.

"No; she could never have reached the shore—that's a fact."

And, deep down in his heart, Jim Madison felt a twinge of regret at the awful fate of the dauntless girl; for, bad man though he was, he loved the proud spirited girl. Now that she was dead—and he felt the guilt of her cruel death resting upon himself—he would have given all his ill-gotten gains to undo the wrong that he had done her.

Now that Edith Beaty was dead, as he all but knew, by his villainous plot to break her proud spirit, to ruin her pure and spotless life, to drag her down to a level with himself—for she had, as he intended she should, scarcely two hours before her desperate attempt to save herself, overheard the conversation between himself and

Fred, detailing their hellish plan to accomplish her ruin —Jim Madison experienced that awful sensation that comes to those who realize they have forfeited all rights among men and all claims before the Almighty.

Now that his beautiful and beloved Edith was lying upon the coral reef in the bottom of the sea, the two fugitives felt that Weston would hound them, and nothing save death would stay his vengeful hand.

"Let us wait till morning and see who they are," said Fred.

Accordingly, they waited till morning and watched for the appearance of the newly married couple, in order to determine their identity before returning to the ship.

At last they appeared, and passed within a few feet of the spot where Jim and Fred, concealed behind the stained glass of a saloon front, stood watching. Consternation seized them when they recognized little Edith Beaty, beautiful and happy, leaning upon the strong arm of Tom Weston.

"Angels and ministers of grace defend us!" breathlessly exclaimed Jim Madison. "Edith and Tom—by the Holy Moses!"

Pale and trembling, he stood and watched them as they passed by.

Fred Wimmer could find no words to express the consternation and horror which seized upon his guilty heart as he beheld alive and well and looking more beautiful than ever the girl for whose cruel death he had felt himself responsible as an accomplice. It seemed to him like the hand of fate—a fate which haunted his guilty conscience with a sickening fear of a certain and a swiftly coming doom.

"In the name of God!" he groaned, as, at last, Fred found utterance for that awful horror which had seized upon his cowardly heart. "Has the sea given up its victim? What shall we do, Jim?" he asked, turning to his

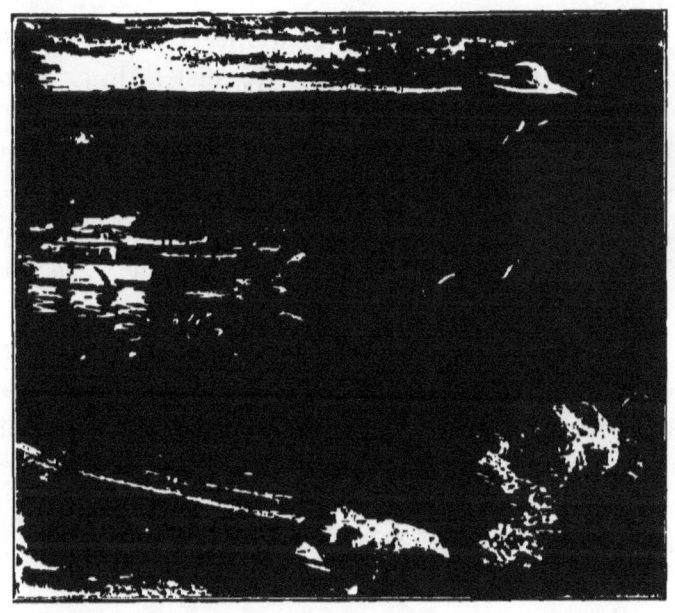

"A Good View of the Harbor Could Be Had."

companion. "Come—arouse yourself! We have no time to lose! We must act at once!"

"Come! We must watch and see if they leave on the ship!" whispered Jim, breathlessly. "If we could only see the captain and tell him that we have made other arrangements—that we can not go with him."

"But we can't do that—so let them go."

"Go?" interrupted Jim, excitedly. "If they only *will* go, we are saved. But will they go? NEVER! For the captain of the City of Brooklyn—honest old duffer!—will send for us, suspicion will be aroused, and that daredevil, Weston, will be on our track in less than two hours from now.

"Yes—some thing must be done, Fred. We must devise some plan to outwit him—to mislead him. Come! Let us watch and see what they do."

Gaining a position from which a good view of the harbor could be had, they watched the ship.

Soon they saw the captain's boat bearing the happy bride and her husband to the ship, and, a little later, they saw the boat return—evidently in search of them.

"They are looking for us," cried Jim, excitedly; "and if I mistake not, Tom Weston is with them. By ——!" hissed Jim, with an oath, "if he is along, there is yet a fighting chance for us! We must manage so as to lead him away from the rest of them, and then send a message to Edith—our old trick. She will bite again."

"Never mind the girl," said Fred. "Let her go, if she will."

"By all the fiends in ——!" cried Jim, exultantly. "Yonder goes Tucson Joe. Quick! Let us overtake the Bad Man from Bitter Creek."

And off they started in pursuit.

In a few minutes they had come up with him, and had enlisted his services in their behalf by the offering of a liberal reward.

"Now to work!" exclaimed Jim. "The first thing is to lead him to a place where we can handle him."

"I know a place," said Tucson Joe, whar we kin do ther job, and fer $500 I 'll put him whar he 'll not pester yer agin. I 've got an ole score ter settle with him, anyhow, and I mout jest as well do both jobs at wunst. So come on down ter my place, and we 'll fix it up."

Leading the way, Tucson Joe piloted Jim and Fred down near the wharves, among the low dives and groggeries that were plentiful there.

Entering a gloomy-looking building, used as a sort of rookery for the nesting of the "wharf rats," the toughs and all such as could not afford, or did not prefer, a better place, they soon found themselves in Tucson Joe's "headquarters."

Vile women, dirty, wretched and ill-clad children and drunken men leered at the strangers as they passed on up and along a rickety flight of stairs to a room in the back part of the building.

"This is my place," said Tucson Joe. "Set down, an' we 'll 'range matters."

"We must work fast," declared Jim. "Weston is on shore, but he may return to the ship with the men any time. We must lure him away from them and get him here before the ship leaves, so we can get the girl."

"I 'll tell yer how we kin manage him," said Tucson Joe. "I 'll meet him, and be talkin' with him 'bout you fellers, an' I 'll git him ter come here, somehow, but I don't know how I 'll do it yet. I 'll have ter see him an' talk with him a leetle before I kin 'range that part of it.

You two fellers—you jest stay here till I report. Yer kin bet I 'll fetch him."

So saying, Tucson Joe left the room. Half an hour later, he met Tom Weston on the street.

"Hello there—Tucson Joe! Where away?" hailed Tom.

"Geewhiliken Moses!" exclaimed Joe, in well feigned surprise. "Like ter knock ther head off 'n me agin—now, would n't yer?"

"No—not unless I had as good a cause as that night at the Casino. But say, Joe, I want to talk with you a little."

"All right, pard—fire away."

"You knew Jim Madison, did n't you?"

"Yes; I knowed him some."

"Well, Joe, there is a reward of $10,000 offered for his arrest. He is at present in this town, and if you can pick him up I will see that you get the money just as soon as you point him out to me or the police."

"Moly Hoses!" cried Joe. "Ten thousand dollars! I 'll jest win that air reward immejitly, or my name ain't Tucson Joe! Say, Tom! By h—, I ain't no perticler friend o' your 'n, but I 've got er leetle racket on hand, and I 'll blow on 'em—durn me if I don't. I know whar Jim and his pard is this very minute, and I wus a-workin' a drive fer 'em. But that ten thousand beats ther devil all outen their offer. Come with me, and I 'll show yer whar they is. Git a pleecemun, ef yer want er."

"Wait for me till I send a note to my wife, to have her come here. Come in until I am ready," said Tom.

Here they entered the Victoria Hotel, where Tom wrote a note to his wife and then sent a carriage to bring her.

"Give this letter to the man in charge of the boat, and tell him to deliver it to the lady on board the City of Brooklyn," said Tom, as the carriage drew up and instructions were asked for.

"Yes, sir," responded the driver, and drove away.

"Now," said Tom, "I am ready."

"Wal, what shell we do?" asked Joe. "Shell we git ther pleece, or take 'em ourselves?"

"We will take them ourselves," replied Tom.

"Wal, jest as yer say; it makes no difference ter me at all," replied Joe, carelessly. "I did n't know but yer mout think that I wus tryin' ter run a drive onter yer."

"If you are, Joe, I will kill you the very instant that I become aware of it," said Tom.

"All right—jest kill er way."

"I am ready. Lead the way," said Tom.

"Foller me, then. It 's er tough place where they air, I kin tell yer," said Joe, as he struck out toward the dock district.

A half mile brought them to the "Rookery," as it was called. Entering the building, Joe led the way to the room. But when he got there a surprise awaited the treacherous Joe.

Treacherous and dishonorable themselves, Jim and Fred distrusted every one else; and they believed that Tucson Joe would betray them if he could make any thing by so doing. The $10,000 reward would be too much of a temptation for him, they believed. At any rate, they dared not trust him. It would suit their purpose if he lured Weston to the place. He could then share Weston's fate.

In the absence of Joe, Jim and Fred had made arrangements with some half-dozen or more toughs that were lounging about the place to capture the two men. They declared that Weston was a detective, and was hunting them for a reward.

Now, these men had almost as good a reason to fear and hate a detective as Jim and Fred had. So, an offer of $500 for the capture of the detective immediately procured the desired assistance of these half-dozen men.

Stationing them in an adjoining room, Jim Madison and his companion in crime awaited the return of Tucson Joe with their victim.

"Stop here," said Joe in a low tone, as they paused before the door of his room, "while I see if every thing is all right."

Just as he uttered these words the opposite door was opened, and six men with drawn revolvers surrounded them, while at the same time the door before which they had stopped opened, and Jim Madison and Fred Wimmer appeared. Pointing to Tom, they shouted:

"There is the detective! Upon him!"

Quick as lightning Tom's revolver flashed, and Tucson Joe threw up his hands and fell to the floor—dead.

Then commenced the desperate and bloody struggle —the struggle of one against eight.

Crippled as Tom was, it required some little time before the eight men could overpower him. But at last, bruised and bleeding from the thugs' cruel blows and exhausted by his desperate efforts to escape, he was borne to the floor—completely overpowered.

"Now, then, we have got him!" shouted Jim, in glee. "Now, what shall we do with him?"

"Put him out of the way! End the business at once!" answered Fred.

"I reckon that is about the only thing we *can* do," replied Jim.

But here an unlooked for obstacle presented itself. One of the men stepped forward and said:.

"'Old hon, my 'arties! Hi 'ave ha word to say 'ere. Hit 's hagainst our principles to murder ha man hafter 'e 's dishabled and captured. We 've got ha place hexpressly designed for the safe keeping of such victims has 'e his, hand we 'll keep 'im huntil ha ransom his hoffered for 'im."

Without further ado, they conveyed him to a dark, close room, which Tom knew must be situated beneath the building.

The room—or dungeon, for, indeed, such it proved to be—was built of brick, arched over head, and had but one door and two small, grated openings, which served for ventilating purposes only. The room was furnished with a bed, a table, two chairs, a lamp and a few books and papers—furnished for the comfort and convenience of the unfortunate victims who should chance to be confined there. This is what Tom saw in that quick, searching glance which he cast about him as he found himself alone.

Well might a man despair under such circumstances. But Tom Weston was not a man who would give up, no matter how insurmountable the opposing obstacles might seem. He immediately set himself to devise a means of escape, hopeless though the task appeared.

CHAPTER XXXIII.

JOHN MASON MEETS ANOTHER MAN WHO CAN ALSO DRIVE A HARD BARGAIN.

In the evening Tom's jailer came and brought his supper. He asked his prisoner if there was any message that he would like to send to friends, hinting to Tom that a ransom might be taken under consideration.

"About how much of a ransom do you expect, sir?" asked Tom.

"Well, I can't 'ardly say has to that just now. You see, there his no particular 'urry habout the matter. Just think the matter over for ha few days, hand see habout what you can hafford to give," said the man, coolly.

"I can send a message then, can I?" asked Tom.

"We 'ave no objection—providing that hit 's hall right," replied the man.

In a few minutes a note was penciled and submitted to the censor, who read it and promised to forward it. But, for some reason, Edith never received her husband's note. Another note, penned by another hand, was substituted for it.

"Tom's Jailer Came and Gave Him His Supper."

The interference of these men, though it ought not to have been entirely unexpected, for both Jim and Fred knew them to be blackmailers, confidence men, burglars—in fact, any thing that would pay them—was so sudden that for a time Jim and his friend were completely at a loss to know what to do or how to proceed. They could ransom their dangerous enemy, but, unfortunately for them, they were short of funds; beside, they were in no little peril themselves.

"We are up a stump!" declared Jim. "The only thing that I know of that we can do now is to prevent Edith from learning any thing about him. If we can so manage as to get hold of her, we can win yet."

"I don't know about that," said Fred, doubtfully. "If we meddle with her, we are liable to get into a snap. Beside, I do not believe that she can be fooled again. Neither do I believe such an effort to be safe. The people at the Victoria Hotel are mightily taken up with her, and, if she should disappear, h—l would be to pay and no pitch hot! Let us stave off the ransom as long as possible. We can tell them that we have money in the United States, and will get it before long. If that is not satisfactory, then threaten to expose them."

"That's just the card!" exclaimed Jim, exultantly. "They dare not make any arrangements with Edith for Weston's ransom. Ours are the winning cards, and we can play them, too!"

"Yes—but how are they to be played?" asked Fred.

"In the first place," said Jim, "we must come to an understanding with those fellows about that ransom affair. After that is disposed of, attention must be paid to the management of the girl."

For several days nothing in particular was done. Tom Weston's custodians had made an offer to deliver him to Jim Madison on receipt of $6,000. This was accepted conditionally, the proviso being that the blacklegs should wait a reasonable period for funds to reach Sidney from their agent in America.

"We will do this," said John Mason, the Englishman, "provided you will pay ha bonus hof $1,000. We 'ave got to 'ave some money hout hof this right haway. We can git hit hof 'im, but we would rather hacommodate you hif we can. You hunderstand our proposition, pard?"

JOHN MASON.

For some time Jim remained silent.

"Do just as you please," said John Mason. "Hit makes no difference to me, honly hi wanted to know at wunst. Weston his gittin' himpatient; 'e 'll come round hin no time."

"Well, I will accept your terms, provided you will let me have the care of the prisoner till I get the money. I must see after him and decide about all communications, and must have the management of him."

"Hi cahn't hagree to that."

"Can't agree to it!" thundered Jim, in a rage as violent as it was sudden. "By the eternal, you shall agree to it! Listen! I am not sure that I can get this money for several months—possibly, not before Spring. But I want to tell you, John Mason, that I have too much at stake to be balked, now that I have trapped my man. I have accepted your *terms*—now you shall accept my *time*. I tell—wait till I am done speaking before you answer—I tell you I will not be balked or thwarted in this! I hold the winning cards, and I will play them, too, if your absorbing greed makes it necessary! I will expose you and bring the police here the very minute that you refuse. Accept my time, and I will pay you $100 per month for keeping him. Refuse, and I will bring the police here within an hour!"

John Mason and his villainous gang had about as much to fear from a visit of the police as Jim and Fred had; and, being a coward, he dared not refuse the proposition. So, after considering the matter and concluding that there was no alternative, John Mason answered:

"Make hit han 'undred hand fifty ha month, hand we will accept hand you can 'ave the management hof 'is business has long has you pay up regular hin hadvance; hand we will 'elp you hall we can beside."

"Done!" exclaimed Jim, extending his right hand.

CHAPTER XXXIV.

WHILE FRED WIMMER INSISTS THAT SOME THING IS UP, HE IS ORDERED TO THROW HIS HANDS UP.

"Now," said Jim, as he and Fred found themselves alone—"now for the girl. We must try some scheme to lure her here."

"Jim, I want to tell you that it won't do for us to fool with that girl. Just as sure as we undertake to meddle with her, we will be up a stump. I will not have any thing to do with her. Just let her stay where she is till Weston is disposed of; then, possibly, you can manage her."

"Well, if we can just manage to keep her quiet for a little while, I'll guarantee that Mr. Tom Weston steps down and out of our way," said Jim.

Thus the plan was laid, and for several months it was carried out to the best of their ability. But matters did not develop to their entire satisfaction, for Tom Weston had not yet "stepped down and out." At last the dark clouds of the gathering storm began to hover about the heads of the two adventurers. The thunder of a just vengeance muttered in a warning tone their pending fate, but they heeded it not.

As the Winter months dragged slowly by—months which to them were months of anxiety, of uncertainty, of danger and dread, and of the deepest fear lest their prisoner should escape, lest Edith's suspicions should be aroused, lest their treacherous accomplices in crime

"Six Masked and Armed Men Entered the Room."

should discover their identity and betray them for the reward—they were so haunted and tormented that they had decided upon a desperate plan to accomplish their ends.

Seven months had passed, and their finances were so nearly exhausted that they could wait no longer without betraying their true condition.

"It is no use," declared Jim. "We must act before another pay day comes around. There is no delaying it any longer."

"But what shall we do?" asked Fred, dubiously. "I don't like this business. You have spent every cent of your money, and have gained nothing. It is no use. I can't throw my money away. I have done all that I can do for you."

"Hold on, Fred!" cried Jim, threateningly. "You are in for this. You can not go back on me at this advanced stage of the game. Wait till I tell you what I propose to do. We must kidnap Edith, and then make Tom come to terms. The first thing that we must do is to give her to understand that we are holding her husband a prisoner some where—say in New York. By the eternal! I wish we had him there instead of here. She will go to New York, and once we get her there I will take care of her all right. We will have to let Tom go. We can't do any thing with him. They will not give him up, and we can not get him. If we could only find the place where he is concealed, things could be managed quite differently; but, in spite of all that I can do, I can not find where he is hidden."

"I tell you, Jim," declared Fred, "that some thing is up. Twice in the last few days I have been dogged here, and I am not going to stay here another day. The men here are up to some thing. I have been warned by a particular friend of mine."

"What were you warned of?" asked Jim.

"That some thing is up. I don't propose to stay and see what it is."

"By ——, but you shall stay here and ——"

Here the door was opened, and six masked and armed men entered the room, closed the door behind them, and demanded in a threatening tone:

"Dogged."

"'Ands hup!" And the ominous click of a half-dozen revolvers emphasized the demand.

Abject cowards as were Jim and Fred, they dared not disobey, and consequently in a moment the two were disarmed. Jim was bound and blindfolded, and then led away raging and fuming in the most abject fear. He first threatened, then begged and finally, all else failing, he burst into tears. Between his sobs he managed to ask where they were taking him.

"For God's sake," he wailed, "don't deliver me up to the police—don't!"

"No use, my 'arty," declared John Mason. "We 'ave struck a better lay."

"But where are you taking me?" asked Jim.

"To the dungeon," replied his captors. "You 'ave been trying to get there for ha long time, so we thought that we would hacommodate you. Furthermore, our old pard, Tom Weston, wants to see you. 'E wants to 'ave ha little chat with you."

"O my God!" wailed Jim, as the horrible truth flashed upon his mind that he had been betrayed. "O my God! Don't take me to him!"

Had they not supported him, Jim Madison would undoubtedly have fallen to the ground from sheer fright. But strong arms carried him down the long, narrow passage to the dungeon, where Tom Weston had spent so many dreary months.

—:o:—

CHAPTER XXXV.

TOM WESTON BAGS HIS GAME, BUT EDITH MYSTERIOUSLY DISAPPEARS FROM HER HOTEL.

Days, weeks and months passed, and the lonely occupant of the dungeon had lost all count of time. Yet he did not despair. When first he found himself a prisoner, he began to cast about him for a means of escape.

But as time dragged heavily on till it lengthened out from days to weeks and from weeks to months without an opportunity of escape offering itself, and as further restraint was becoming unbearable, Tom determined on a bold and reckless plan of escape.

He had learned that he owed his long imprisonment solely to Jim Madison, and he resolved not only to make his escape, but to have revenge.

Nearly eight months had passed since that fateful day when he entered the old "Rookery," and all this time he had been waiting. Now, he believed, the time had come for him to act. The men were dissatisfied with Jim, and lately they had detected him in his efforts to locate the dungeon. So, in consequence of all this, Tom began feeling his way. Slowly and cautiously he proceeded at first, but when he had satisfied himself that the coast was clear, he came out boldly with his offer, which was accepted readily.

He told them of the $10,000 reward offered for the arrest of Jim Madison, and added:

"IN AN INSTANT TOM WAS BESIDE HER."

"Bring Jim Madison here and leave him with me till I can arrange the matter with my wife. She has got the money, and will pay the reward."

But here arose a new difficulty. If they were to let him go, there would still be a chance for Edith to prosecute them.

They must first see her, and make arrangements with her about it; but Tom would not hear to this. He was bound to punish them for the suffering which they had brought upon his little wife. Although he had agreed not to prosecute them himself, he was resolved that his wife should be at liberty to enter proceedings against them. With this object in view, he had decided upon a plan. Desperate though it was, he was fully determined to carry it out. So he gave them to understand that he would accede to their terms.

"Deliver Jim Madison to me at least a week before you make any attempt to arrange the other matter," said Tom. "I want to settle a little matter between us."

"Hall right," said John Mason, and left him.

Not long after, Jim Madison, pale and almost fainting from the horror of meeting the man whom he had so greatly wronged, was brought to the dungeon.

"Ah, Jim, my dear friend! I am so very, *very* glad to meet you!" exclaimed Tom. "What? Have you no word of greeting?" he asked in a low, deep tone that quivered with the awful passion that raged within him. "Sit down, my dear boy! I want to talk with you."

Tom told him of the murder of old John Beaty, of the mother's death, of the noble girl's work, of the finding of the murdered man's remains and the knife, of their long pursuit, of his base and vile treatment of Edith, of the reason why she had made the desperate effort to get ashore from his vessel in the face of the storm which she knew to be approaching, and last, if not least, of the misery brought upon her by the uncertain fate of her husband.

For three days Tom Weston lingered about his victim. He did him no violence, yet in those three days Jim Madison was made to suffer the torments of a thousand deaths.

Haggard and almost bereft of his reason, he sank down in a fit at the end of the third day, and was unconscious when John Mason, the jailer, brought them their supper.

This was the opportunity for which Tom had worked and waited. Nerving himself for the ordeal, he waited for Mason to enter.

"'Ello 'ere!" exclaimed the jailer, as his eyes fell on the prostrate Jim—convulsed and foaming at the mouth. "'E 's got 'em this time, sure enough!"

These words were scarcely out of John Mason's mouth when, with a bound, Tom sprang upon him and seized him by the throat. Then for a few moments followed a desperate and savage struggle—a struggle that could only end with the life of one of the contestants. Tom's iron grip never relaxed its hold on his antagonist's throat till, black and quivering, he lay still—as Tom believed and intended—in death.

"Now for the next!" muttered Tom, as he appropriated Mason's revolver and knife. These weapons were duly examined and properly bestowed.

Going to the door, Tom gave the same signal that he had seen Mason give so many times before. Immediately the door opened, and before the man who had been left there could cry out or resist Tom dealt him a crushing blow full over the right temple with the butt end of his revolver, and he fell heavily on the floor, quivering in death.

Tom dragged the man inside the dungeon and closed and securely locked the door.

"Tom Sprang Upon Him."

"There! For a little while I will play keeper myself."

Turning to leave the loathsome den, he found himself in a dark, narrow passage at the foot of a long and rickety flight of stairs that were so narrow and steep he could with difficulty ascend.

Picking his way slowly along, he climbed up what seemed to him the space of two stories, when he came to a half-open door that opened into a small bed room.

Approaching the door cautiously, he beheld before him and sitting with her back toward him a rather graceful and stylish young lady, who was deeply interested in the absorbing and enchanting plot of a late French yellow back novel. In an instant Tom was at her side, and in a tone of stern command he said:

"Silence! I will not harm you. Come with me, and lead me out of this robbers' roost! Pilot me to the street, and I'll let you go. Not a word—on your life! Lead the way!"

Obeying, she led him down a long and shaky flight of stairs, at the foot of which she opened a door and said in apparent unconcern:

"This leads to the street. Will you send the police here?"

"Why do you ask?'

"That I may avoid them," she replied.

"Go, then; for the police will be here within an hour at farthest," said Tom, as he disappeared in the darkness.

It was ten o'clock when he reached the police station and reported the case. He also gave the officer in charge directions for locating the dungeon.

"Is this Tom Weston?" inquired the police captain.

"Yes."

"Your wife was here yesterday. I think she started for New York this morning."

"My God!"

Without another word, Tom started on a run for the Victoria Hotel. Reaching that hostelry, he learned that Edith had departed at ten o'clock that very morning for New York.

"So near and yet so far! O God! Why could n't I have been a little sooner!" moaned Tom.

"Is there any thing that I can do for you, Mr. Weston?" asked the proprietor.

"No—nothing! Yes! When is there a vessel for New York?'

"In four days!"

"Four days! And must I wait all that time?"

"You will not lose much by it," said the proprietor, "for the steamer that leaves here four days hence gets into port at New York only twelve hours later than the one upon which your wife sailed."

Half an hour later, a telegram reached Sidney, saying that the Sea Nymph—the vessel upon which Edith sailed—had been driven upon the rocks and was lost.

The passengers and crew were, except three, saved—so, at least, stated the telegram. Then followed the list of the missing, but Edith's name did not appear among them.

Anxiously hoping that he might be so fortunate as to reach the scene of the disaster before Edith should leave, Tom set out immediately and with all haste for the place where the wreck occurred. He arrived there at four o'clock the next evening.

Searching diligently among the survivors and shore men, he was at last rewarded by what he hoped would prove a valuable clew. At any rate, the description answered very well.

"But this air wor a boy," persisted the old shore man whom Tom had questioned.

"She may be disguised as a boy ——"

"Wal, I swow!" broke in the old man.

"She is not very large; rather slim; dark-blue eyes; hair short and curly; quite pretty." Tom gave this description with evident pride.

"This air gal—if it be a gal—wor not so very slim; but she wor purty as a pictur, and she saved a baby's life what was drifting away."

"And she went to San Francisco, you say?" queried Tom.

"She said she wor goin' thar, but she wor goin' tew Farmingtown from here. She 'll have tew wait thar till a steamer goes tew 'Frisco," said the shore man.

"Well, to Farmingtown I 'll go. Maybe, I can overtake her there," said Tom.

On reaching the place, he was again disappointed; for the person he described had left, not six hours before, for New York, by way of Yokohama and San Francisco Fortunately a steamer, the Golden Gate, had just the touched at the pier on her way to San Francisco direct. Tom barely had time to secure passage.

In due time he arrived at San Francisco and looked about for Edith.

On inquiring at the ticket office, he learned that a boy answering to his description had purchased a ticket there, and had started for New York scarcely two hours before.

"I want to send a message to a person on that train," said Tom. He dictated the message and awaited results. In the land of the telegraph—the home land of the telegraph—one seldom waits long.

"What Is It?" Asked the Girl.

CHAPTER XXXVI.

EDITH REJOINS HER HUSBAND, AND A THIRD AND INTERESTING PARTY JOINS THE HAPPY COUPLE.

"Oh, I can not stand this any longer!" exclaimed the unhappy Edith. "I will search for Tom—I will find my noble, loving husband!"

Dissuasion and remonstrance of friends fell on deaf ears.

Disguising herself in boy's attire—as she had often done before—she went among the dark dens of vice, wretchedness and crime along the docks and adjacent streets.

Here among the toughs, blacklegs and the lowest and most wretched scum of a great city's population, she toiled and worked with that undaunted courage and unceasing and persistent energy which had borne her so triumphantly through many dark and desperate struggles. Here she had dogged the footsteps of Fred Wimmer even to the very door of the house where Tom, in his dark and dreary dungeon, was perfecting his plan of escape.

One day, along toward evening, she had trailed her victim to the docks, where he had gone to the ticket office and purchased a ticket for New York, and then had gone aboard the steamer. There his impatience tortured him as he waited to sail, for he had not felt safe since his discovery that he was being shadowed.

Following him aboard the great ship, Edith pointed out Fred Wimmer to the police officer, who attempted to place him under arrest. Fred resisted the officer, and was shot dead.

Thus the lips that might have revealed the whereabouts of Tom Weston and Jim Madison were for ever sealed in death.

All further search failed to turn up anything concerning either Tom or Jim. Edith became convinced that her husband was slain, and resolved to avenge his death, if possible.

Now that Fred was dead, all hope of gaining any information from him vanished, of course. But there was one erroneous conclusion which Fred's actions had led Edith to form. She argued that, as Fred was going to New York, Jim Madison was either with him or had preceded him. She could never have guessed the cause of their separation.

She could see nothing for her to do, except to extend her pursuit of Jim to New York. With this purpose in mind, she embarked on the Sea Nymph.

The day of Edith's departure from Sidney dawned beautiful and full of promise, and the proud ship bounded lightly over the shining sea on her course, bearing her burden of precious human lives.

Twelve hours later, a dense fog enveloped them, and the proud ship struck upon some hidden rocks and went down. So sudden was her sinking, there was scarcely time for the boats to be manned and the passengers to be taken off.

Edith was fortunate in being among the first batch of passengers taken off the sinking ship, and still more so in securing passage to a small town on the coast. Here she caught a regular line steamer for San Francisco, and reached the Sunset City after a pleasant voyage.

Arriving at San Francisco, she immediately repaired to the railroad depot and bought a ticket for New York City. She entered the train at the earliest moment possible and impatiently awaited its departure for the East. At the minute scheduled the train pulled out and went flying away up the great Sacramento valley.

"Settled Herself for a Long Ride."

Well nigh exhausted by her long sea voyage, Edith settled herself down as comfortably as possible for the long ride across the continent.

On thundered the train, seemingly at lightning speed —on through the beautiful Valley of the Sacramento— then struck boldly out across the country and began to climb the great Sierras.

Here, nestling in a pleasant little valley, was a small village, and here the train stopped for a few minutes.

Scarcely had the train stopped when the telegraph operator handed a message to the conductor, and asked him to go through the coaches and read it aloud, so that if the person for whom it was intended was aboard she would hear it read.

As the conductor entered the coach in which Edith was riding he read the telegram, and was about to pass on, as no response was made, when he noticed the rather attractive-looking figure of Edith, who happened to be asleep at the time.

"Here, my lad—wake up!" said the conductor, shaking her gently.

"What is it?" asked the startled girl.

"See if this interests you," said the conductor, and he read:

"EDITH WESTON: Return to the Golden Gate Hotel, San Francisco. TOM."

"At last! At last! O thank God!" cried the girl, joyously.

"You will stop here," said the conductor, for he saw that his strange passenger was not only deeply moved by the message, but was a remarkably beautiful young lady in disguise. "There will be a train going back in fifteen minutes upon which you can go."

"I thank you for waking me, sir," said Edith, as she left the train.

Fifteen minutes later, she started back for the Golden Gate.

Bounding down the mountain slope, then dashing away across the country; now down the broad Sacramento, and finally coming to a stop in the great railway depot of the Sunset City—thus flew the anxious, loving wife to meet her faithful husband.

As Edith stepped from the train and cast an eager, expectant glance over the crowd of people, she saw the broad shoulders and well known form of Tom Weston, as he paced back and forth, scanning the faces of the passengers in evident anxiety.

A light hand rested upon his arm, and, turning, he beheld the boy described by the old Australian shore man.

"Edith!"

And, all unmindful of the vast crowd of curious people who surged about him, he folded the slight form in his strong arms.

"Tom!" cried Edith, joyously.

"Hack, sir?"

"Yes. To the Golden Gate."

Three weeks had passed, and on this beautiful Spring morning Tom Weston was made doubly happy. During the night a wee creature, as if borne from Heaven upon angel wings, had paused in her flight and rested upon the fair, warm bosom of the happy little wife and doting mother—Edith Weston. Such a wee thing it was, and so delicate and beautiful, that one could scarcely feel convinced that it was really a mortal and belonged to the earth. Happy Edith! Never was a mother more demonstrative in her transports of joy.

"O Tom!" murmured Edith, as she felt his warm kiss upon her pale cheek. "God has rewarded me again for all my sufferings—for all my troubles and disappointments. "See, Tom!" And she showed him their little treasure.

"But, Tom"—and her fine eyes, filled with tears of joy, dilated and for a moment that strange, wild look which he had seen there so many times before flashed from them as she asked the question—"do you know any thing of Jim Madison?"

"I won't tell you now, Edith," answered Tom. "By-and-by, I will tell you all about it. Just as soon as you are able, we will go down to Los Angeles and look up the little home that we were talking about so long ago. We have got the happy little family now, and, to make the dream complete, we must have the little home."

—:o:—

"OH! WHAT A LOVELY PLACE!"

CHAPTER XXXVII.

EDITH ACKNOWLEDGES THE REALIZATION OF HER GIRLHOOD'S BRIGHTEST DREAMS.

Two months after the meeting of Tom and Edith at San Francisco, Tom received a letter from police headquarters at Sidney, stating that two weeks after he left for America John Mason's dungeon was discovered. Jim Madison, reduced to a skeleton by starvation and bereft of reason by the awful torment which had racked his soul, was found within it, together with the dead bodies of two men, upon whose rotting flesh he was at the time of his discovery feasting.

"O Tom!" cried Edith, as he finished reading the letter. "What an awful retribution! How terribly he must have suffered! Tell me all about it, Tom."

"All right, Kid; I will tell you."

Tom then told his wife in detail the story of dreary months passed in the dungeon—of his plan for vengeance and his desperate fight for liberty.

"Yes," he continued, "I left him there. I intended that he should suffer, but not quite so much nor so long. I did not know whether the other two men were dead; neither did I care. Horrible! Horrible! How he must have suffered! Twelve days! Indeed, he had plenty of time to think over his wicked life—to think of each separate crime he had committed. Ah! I wonder if he remembered the Kid? I wonder if he remembered little

Edith? I wonder if he remembered her murdered father and worse than murdered mother? I wonder if he then remembered the vile insults—his fiendish plot to break her proud spirit, to ruin the pure life of his little captive—and, last, the long months of suffering which he had brought upon her by depriving her of her husband at a time when, above all others, she most needed his care and protection? Horrible as his suffering must have been, I think it was merited."

"Yes—it was indeed awful!" said the proud little mother, as she pressed to her heart her newly found and greatly prized treasure. "But, Tom, what is to be done with him now? Have they sent for instructions concerning him?"

"Yes. They want to know what is to be done with him. I think we should let him remain where he is till he has recovered his reason—if he ever does. Then he shall be brought here and turned over to the proper civil authorities. His must be a life-long punishment."

And so, as it was decided to let him remain, instructions were sent and all necessary arrangements made for his comfort and medical treatment at the asylum for the insane.

"Now," said Tom, after this business was attended to, "we will go and look at that place that I was telling you of when we were at Los Angeles."

"Perhaps it is sold before now," said Edith. "We promised to go and look at it in a few days. That was a year ago."

"Oh, there is not the least danger that it has been

sold. We will go and look at it and see how you like its location and surroundings."

Three days later, Tom and Edith found themselves again in Los Angeles.

Paying a visit to the land agent, they made arrangements with him about the property, a description of which had so greatly pleased Edith the year before.

"I will drive you out any day," said the agent, "and let Mrs. Weston see for herself. It is the best place that I have the care of at present; in fact, it is the most desirable location that I know of."

The place proved to be fully up to the highest expectations of the home seekers—a veritable paradise.

A beautiful little cottage situated near a small inlet—too small to be a refuge for large vessels, but making a safe and beautiful harbor for the pleasure boats of the villagers—upon the gently sloping hillside, overlooking the bay and the little village upon the opposite shore, while away in the distance, over a stretch of some half-dozen miles of rolling fields, orchards, vineyards and gardens, dotted here and there with groves of oranges and olives and towering evergreens, and the giant oaks, whose dark and variegated foliage painted the landscape in beautiful tints of green and gold—beyond these lay the placid waters of the Pacific Ocean, upon whose level surface floated stately ships from every nation, and innumerable white-winged coasting vessels and craft of all descriptions flitted restlessly or lay basking in the warm sun like things of life and beauty.

Behind rose the sloping hills, upon whose sunny sides

the orange groves and vineyards painted pictures of purple and gold, and in whose valleys nestled the beautiful cottage homes of many prosperous and happy families.

"What a lovely place!" exclaimed Edith, as she stood on the vine-covered porch of her future home and surveyed, with a feeling of rapture almost approaching perfect bliss, the surrounding scenery.

"Nothing could be more beautiful and home-like," declared the agent. "This place was laid out for a home, but disappointment—not misfortune—robbed its owner of the privilege of enjoying it. The gardens are the best to be found in California. The orchards and vineyards contain the finest qualities of fruits. But one improvement could be made, although for you it would at present be unnecessary, and that is a larger house."

"I would not have it larger," declared Edith. "It is plenty large— just right as it is."

"Well, Kid, if it suits, you may consider it yours," said Tom. "Here we will make our future home."

"O Tom! Are you quite sure that we can afford it? We have spent so much money in our search——"

"It's all right, my little wife," said Tom. "This is our home henceforth. So be at ease about the payment for it; that is already provided for."

Within a few days Tom and Edith were comfortably settled in their new home.

The little house had been fully furnished, in anticipation of its future mistress, and all was ready, when she should come, for her to go directly to housekeeping.

Nothing could be more cheery and home-like than

the little cottage, with its gardens teeming with a profusion of the most exquisite flowers.

"A veritable little paradise!" exclaimed Edith, as, radiant with the happiness which filled her heart, she came and sat beside Tom in a large rustic chair, on the porch, over which the honeysuckle and rose, loaded with a countless number of sweet-scented flowers, trailed their long lengths, forming a bower variegated with green, scarlet and gold.

"A perfect little Eden! Don't you think so, Tom?" asked Edith.

"All but the serpent, Kid."

THE COTTAGE.

"Tom, this is the fulfillment of my girlish dreams. I have dreamed of happiness like this; I have dreamed of a beautiful little home; and I have dreamed of a kind, noble, true-hearted man, Tom, like you, to take me to his heart and call me his little wife. Further, I have dreamed of a sweet little flower—like our own precious Angel—who came to bind our hearts still closer in love and constancy. I have dreamed of all this, Tom, in my girlhood dreams. And now, Tom, my dreams are realized and I am so happy! Oh, so happy!

"But, Tom, how sad must be the one who planned all these beautiful things, and worked for so many years to make such a lovely home, now that a cruel fate has driven him away! Perhaps he is now too old to build and thus embellish another home, and views with envy the happiness of the more fortunate one who enjoys the fruits of his labor. Do you know the poor man, Tom?"

A smile of triumph played on Tom Weston's plain, honest face as he answered the question asked by his tender-hearted wife:

"Yes, Kid, I know the man. I know him very well, indeed."

"Tell me of him, Tom, and the story of this place; for I know that it must have a romance attached to it."

"Really, Kid, I am not sure that I ought to do so," said Tom.

"Please do, Tom—won't you?"

When he looked down into those wide, pleading eyes, so full of love and pity, he answered:

"My little girl, it was I who built this home."

"O Tom!" cried Edith. "You? Tell me, Tom—tell me all about it."

"Dare I to do this, Edith? Dare I tell you all?"

"Nonsense, Tom! You know that you dare to tell me all, for you are a gentleman."

"I Pleaded. I Promised to Toil for Her."

CHAPTER XXXVIII.

TOM WESTON RECITES TO EDITH THE STORY OF HIS FIRST LOVE DREAM—THE POVERTY TEST.

"Well," said Tom, meditatively, "I came here ten years ago and bought this place. I went to work, with all the energy and ambition of a very ambitious young man, to build me a home and at the same time to win me a wife. Don't look at me that way, Kid, or I will back out and not tell my story. With what success I built my home you can judge for yourself. But the second part of the task—the winning of a wife—well, I will tell you about her; then you can judge of that, too. Of course, this is what you want to know.

"I was pretty well off—rich, perhaps, you may call it—and a little bit romantic as well; or, at any rate, I had notions of my own, and one of these notions was to marry for love. I must love the girl who was to be my wife, and she must love me. I managed my own love affair as I thought it would best suit my notion—that is, as I believed would thoroughly test the love for me of my betrothed wife. And this is how I managed it:

"Remember, we were engaged to be married, and of course the wedding was to be a grand affair, for we were both wealthy. That was three years ago.

"I arranged my affairs so as to make it appear that a great financial misfortune had befallen me. Maybe it was wrong for me to do so, but I do not always stop to consider whether a thing is right or wrong before I act. I wanted to know whether the girl loved me or not—whether she would marry me because I was an agreeable mate or simply sought my fortune, the fine home and the finery which my money would buy for her. And that is why I did it. All my large fortune, my lands, farms and vineyards—all were gone, and I was left penniless. I found myself well nigh friendless as well. And this was the result:

"I went out to work as a common laborer to earn my daily bread, and then I sought, for the first time in my poverty, the presence of my affianced wife.

"The Girl Who Was to Be My Wife."

This was just one week before the day set for our wedding. I sent her my card and waited in the magnificent parlor of her elegant home till she came. Beautiful as ever—yes, she is called a beauty. She yet lives just over there," and he pointed out her residence. "You will see her before long. But I am digressing.

"She met me, and I—poor fool!—mistook the look of pity in her dark eyes for the love-light of former days. But alas for my confidence, never too great! She greeted me as though I were a stranger, and before I left her I *was* a stranger.

"She said: 'Yes—we must part; it is better so. Henceforth we are strangers.'

"I pleaded; I promised to toil for her. But all my pleading was in vain. With a cold and haughty bow, she turned and left me—on my knees and in tears.

"I was young then—only twenty—and possibly I did love her at that time; but I could not love her now. I thank God that she is not my wife instead of you, Kid. Now you can judge."

"Oh, you are safe in my hands, Tom. You know I could not judge you any thing but a brave, noble boy."

While the happy little wife spoke, a shudder of dread passed over her, as though the shadow of some horrible dream enveloped her, while her wondering eyes looked up into his with that expression of fright which he had seen there many times before.

"But, Tom, if you had married her, what would have become of me? Just think of the past two years—of the time when you first met me. O Tom! What would have become of me?"

"'Tis said, Edith, God cares for His children."

"And I believe it, Tom."

CHAPTER XXXIX.

A LETTER FROM FAR-OFF AUSTRALIA BRINGS THE NEWS THAT JIM MADISON IS AT LARGE.

"Tom, do you know that there are a few things that have happened to me in the past two years which make me believe that God, in some way, has watched over me—has heard my prayers and answered them? I have at times thought that I must be wicked; that God had forsaken me and left me to the mercy of my enemies; and I have thought it hard and cruel that I should be compelled to suffer as I have suffered. But when I come to look back and see it all at a glance, I can see things that I had forgotten—things which banish all doubt from my mind and heart as the mist is dispelled before the morning sun. Tom, what would have become of me had you married Belle Winslow? Did you ever think of it, Tom? Just look back from the present to that evening at the Casino! Ah, you will say, Tom, that it was all mere chance—just happened so. Perhaps it did, Tom; but if so, it was a lucky chance for me. I understand now the cause of your aversion to girls, but it was unkind of you to condemn them all because one had proven false to you. There are many brave and true-hearted girls, as well as brave and true-hearted boys, and you will find them every where. I suppose you are acquainted with nearly all the people here, Tom?"

"Yes—all the old settlers. We will have plenty of

"NOT A BIT LIKE HER FATHER"

company here. You will like many of the neighbors, but some you will not," said Tom.

"Not many, I hope," said Edith.

"No—not many. I can name one, and that one is Belle Winslow."

"Why, Tom! Why do you say that?"

"Because she will hate you. If she should think you to be of a jealous disposition, Kid, she would try hard to make you jealous of me. She will try, anyway," said Tom, vehemently.

"But she can't do it, Tom!"

"Of course not. But look, Kid! Some one is coming. They are the Winslows, I see."

A carriage just then turned down the winding, oak-lined avenue which skirted the orange groves and vineyards at the head of the little bay, beyond which the tall gables of the Winslow mansion could be plainly seen, and drove rapidly along the gravel road toward the little cottage known as Cliffside—a name suggested by the high cliff just back of the house.

At the foot of this grim, old cliff, which reared its verdure-clad head hundreds of feet skyward, and upon whose inaccessible and perpendicular face grew trailing vines, nestled the little cottage home like the cozy nest of mating birds.

Dashing swiftly up to the flowery arch of the gateway leading to the front porch, the carriage stopped and a slight, girlish figure dressed in silks and decked with rich jewels alighted and stepped daintily toward the vine-covered porch where Tom and Edith were sitting, and where little Angie, lying in her mother's lap, was receiving the homage usually accorded the first-born.

Tom arose and with a pleasant smile and bow of greeting introduced the young lady to his wife.

Pleasant and cheerful indeed was the greeting which Edith gave her. The two girls chatted away together as only two girls know how to chat for ten minutes or more.

"Oh, what a sweet little baby!" exclaimed Belle, in raptures. "What is her name and how old is she?"

"We call her Angie, and she is twelve weeks old," answered Edith.

"She looks like you, Mrs. Weston—not a bit like— like her father," declared Belle.

"*I* think she looks like Tom," said Edith, resolutely.

"Not the least bit in the world!" imperiously insisted Belle. And from that moment Belle Winslow and Edith Weston were, though secretly, bitter enemies.

"His child!" muttered Belle as she was driven home. "His child! A girl who will dress up in men's clothes and go to saloons and gambling houses, and perhaps— yes, more than likely—to some other places, too, and at night! Ah, well! Maybe she is, but I doubt it. We shall see, Master Tom!"

"I don't like her!" exclaimed Edith with emphasis, as the girl swept down the gravel walk, her silken train rustling in the soft breeze as she entered her elegant carriage and was driven away.

"I knew that you would n't!" declared Tom, with a laugh.

"Tom!" exclaimed Edith, in a tone of reproach, as

she raised her lustrous blue eyes to his, with a look that expressed a complexity of emotions.

"But I did, Kid, and I told you so. You two girls can never be friends, and the less you have to do with each other the better will it be for you, Kid. Of course, you will treat her well, and never show her your dislike."

"But I don't like her!" insisted Edith. "She means some thing by what she said about little Angie. She means mischief. I know that from the look in her black eyes. What did she mean by saying that Angie don't look a bit like you, when I know that she does?"

"It is a very small thing to quarrel over, anyway," said Tom, patting the round, dimpled cheeks of little Angie—"a very small thing."

"It is not what she said, but the way she said it. I tell you, Tom, that girl means mischief."

"What can she do? What do you think she is up to, Kid?"

"I am not sure, Tom, but I will tell you just what I think about it."

In a low tone, quivering with emotion, her dark eyes flashing, she told Tom her fears.

"Nonsense, Kid! Let her talk, if she wants to talk; she can do you no harm. I hope she will not prove so unlady-like and shameless. But, of course, as she is a woman, we will have to let her talk if she will."

"I don't know why, Tom, but I am afraid of her."

"Afraid? And is this my little heroine? Is this the girl who has braved the dangers of sea and storm and defied and routed her enemies? Afraid of that girl?"

"Never mind, Tom. I see that you do not understand me - or, rather, will not admit that you do. Come; let us go down to the shore. The tide is out now. Let us go and see what we can find."

Down they went along the sloping sands until they came up to the boat house, built in a little cove whose waters laved the foot of the cliff, and then along under the great cliff wall, where, at low water, a narrow ledge ran along beneath the overhanging rocks, leading into a little grotto, water-worn and studded with stalactites that were tinted with all the colors of the rainbow.

THE GROTTO

"Oh, what a beautiful place!" exclaimed Edith. "A lovers' retreat—the home of sea nymphs and fairies! Our mortal life must be commonplace beside theirs!"

Thus from one fairy scene to another Tom Weston led his delighted wife as the happy days passed by.

Then came the Autumn season, with its bountiful treasures of luscious fruits and golden grain, bringing wealth and comfort to many happy homes. Bountiful indeed had the harvest been, and the tillers of the soil reaped rich reward for their toil during the Summer.

In these returns of Mother, Earth—these responses to the skill and industry of the husbandmen—Tom and Edith had received their full share, and their happiness seemed limited only by their capacity to enjoy.

Occasionally a letter came from the far-off land of Australia, telling of the progress of Jim Madison toward recovery. . But now a letter came which brought most unwelcome news concerning him.

The letter stated that Jim Madison had made his escape from the insane asylum, and had, up to the time the letter was written, succeeded in eluding the police. No trace of him could be found, but it was believed that he had gone to America.

—:o:—

CHAPTER XL.

THE UNHAPPY LOT OF THE HEAD WHICH HAS A PRICE SET UPON IT.

"Escaped! Jim Madison escaped from the asylum!" exclaimed Edith, nervously, and a shudder passed over her as she thought of what he might possibly attempt to do. Half crazy as he was, he would be far more wily and dangerous than he was before.

"Tom, there is no telling what his insane fancy may prompt him to do."

"It matters not, Edith, whether he may attempt to do any thing. He must be hunted down and punished for the wrong he has already done. I will advertise for him and offer a reward."

This was done without loss of time. Thus, once more, a price was set upon the guilty man's head.

Go where he would, some one would be looking for him, some one would be waiting and watching to receive him. Neither peace nor security could he find, and his guilty conscience would continually harass him. He would see an enemy in every passing face.

"Oh, what a wretched life such an existence must be!" sighed Edith. "To think that all the world is against him; that every one looks upon him as an enemy to be shunned, to be got rid of; an object in whose very misfortune, captivity and punishment other people will find relished profit!"

"Skimming Like a White-Winged Bird."

Edith's revery was interrupted by the approach of a welcome visitor.

"Ah! Here comes some one. I wonder who can she be? Oh, I believe she is that dear old Granny Jones. She was here yesterday, Tom, and was telling me what Belle Winslow has been saying. I told you that Belle would tell it. I knew by the way she looked that she was up to some thing. She is telling it all over the neighborhood. She says that we are not married at all. And do you know, Tom, I lost our marriage certificate? We have nothing to show that we are married, and she seems to know that."

"We have got this little fellow," said Tom, proudly, as he held up little Angie. "See, Kid! What more do you want?"

"It is n't I, Tom; but, you know, Belle says that Angie does n't belong to you."

"Great God! Edith, has that devil-cat been saying such a thing?" cried Tom, white with passion.

"Did n't I tell you, Tom, that she would tell it? Yes—she has told it, and she says, too, that she can prove it. Do you know how she proposes to do this? I will tell you."

In a low voice—her cheeks blushing crimson and her eyes flashing—she repeated to her angered husband the story told openly by Belle Winslow.

Weston was now wild with just indignation.

"D—n her shameless heart! By thunder, if she were only a man! Kid, why don't you jump onto her and give her a trouncing? You can lick a dozen of ——"

"For shame, Tom! But here comes Granny Jones. O Granny!"

The girlish little woman ran to the old lady, grasped her wrinkled hand, kissed her pale cheek and bade her a welcome there was no mistaking.

"O Granny, I am so glad you came over!"

"Ah," said the old lady, gazing down into those blue eyes which greeted her with such welcome. "You are looking happy to-day, my child, and right glad I am to see you looking so well. Oh, and here is little Angie—the sweet little fairy!"

Granny Jones picked up the precious little morsel from her baby-couch and crooned

GRANNY JONES.

to her as fondly and lovingly as though the babe were her daughter's child.

"Sit down, Grandma," said Tom, as he placed the great arm chair before her. "You are well, I see, and the rest of the folk—how are they?" he asked, cheerily.

"All are well, thank you—quite well."

"And so they say, Grandma, that the people over

there [Tom pointed toward the Winslow mansion] are trying to convince our neighbors that little Angie does n't belong to us--or to me, at least. I wonder if they will not try to make out that she does n't belong to Edith, either?"

"No—no!" replied the old lady. "That would not suit their purpose at all. Their sole aim is to injure Edith. Belle Winslow will never forgive you, Mr. Weston, for giving Cliffside to another."

"Nor do I want her to forgive me," declared Tom, emphatically. "I thank God that she is not the mistress of my home!"

From this the conversation changed off to more congenial topics. Granny Jones was high-minded and sympathetic, and her fondness for Edith and Angie made her an ever welcome visitor.

Thus the happy days passed till the Winter months —scarcely distinguishable from those of Summer—had come and gone, and the return of Spring again clothed the hills and vales with luxurious verdure and radiant flowers.

Life at Cliffside was peaceful and happy. Edith and little Angie were known and loved by every one—every one, save only Belle Winslow and a few of her admirers. These must be excepted, for in the heart of Belle Winslow still rankled that bitter feeling of jealous hatred that she bore little Edith for having, as she claimed, robbed her of Cliffside.

"Oh, it 's her beautiful face and fascinating eyes!" declared Belle, resentfully.

In spite of Belle's evil and scandalous tongue, Edith was very happy in the love and care of her little home and family—a fact which was still more exasperating and intolerable to Belle, for she counted upon making Edith miserable.

With the balmy days of Spring began picnics and excursions. A grand picnic to the Santa Barbara Islands was planned for the first of May, which was to be a three days' romp over the islands.

"Oh, won't it be jolly fun!" exclaimed Edith, in her gleeful anticipations.

"It is May Day, you know," joined a half-dozen girls in chorus, "and you must be our May Queen, Edith."

"No," remonstrated Edith. "Choose Belle. You want a girl; choose her."

"She is older than you are, Edith. You are more of a girl than she is," persisted the girls. "You are as like a girl as any of us, and we want you. You are the very prettiest ——"

"There—there, girls! That will do, now," interrupted Tom, who appeared unexpectedly upon the scene. "You can not have my girl. No remonstrance, if you please. Belle Winslow must be your May Queen. It is her right, you know. She always has been, and certainly expects to be again."

"You hear that, girls?" said Edith, taking sides with Tom. "When this chap says 'No'—why, 'No' it is.

"Come, now, girls. Settle upon Belle; crown her Queen of May. It will save some jealous feelings, and that is worth a little sacrifice, especially on such an occasion as this is to be. We want every one to be happy and enjoy the outing to the utmost. If you were to slight Belle in this respect, she would be miserable, and she would then try to make others miserable, too."

"Oh, well! If it is going to spoil any one's pleasure, we won't do it," said the girls.

So it was decided. And when the appointed day came—the first day of May—all the young people and many of the older ones, light hearted and gay, assembled on the village wharf, ready for the start.

"Cliffside," a pretty little pleasure yacht belonging to Tom and Edith, loaded with its freight of laughing girls and boys, took the lead, and was soon skimming over the waters like a white-winged bird.

Happy and gay, with songs and merry jests, the sail to the picnic grounds was enjoyed by all.

—:o:—

CHAPTER XLI.

A MAY-DAY EXCURSION LEAVES CLIFFSIDE AND IS ATTENDED BY A CERTAIN PERUVIAN GENTLEMAN.

Reaching the islands after a short and pleasant sail, the happy picnickers landed upon the rocky shore and immediately began preparations for a good time.

Dinner was the first thing on the program, and ere long little groups of rollicking boys and bright-eyed girls were gathered about here and there, making merry over their bountiful repast.

"Oh, this is just lovely!" exclaimed Edith—her cheeks flushed with pleasure, her dark eyes sparkling with the happiness that filled her heart. "Oh, this is just lovely! A little like camping out, is n't it, Tom?"

"Just a little," replied Tom. "But, say, Kid, who is that long-bearded, foreign-looking gentleman over there with the Winslows? He is a stranger, and, judging from his attentions to Belle, he is badly gone on her."

"Handsome, is n't he?" asked Edith, obeying the woman's instinct of her heart by noticing, first of all, his good looks. "Senor Don Somebody, I expect."

"I wonder if they won't introduce him to us? I saw him looking over here a little while ago, and he seemed to be asking about us," said Tom.

"Tom, I have seen that man before!"

The flush upon Edith's fair cheek gave way to death-like pallor.

"What is the matter? What do you mean, Edith?"

The Picnic on Santa Barbara Islands

asked Tom, who was becoming excited over the sudden change in his wife's countenance.

"Oh, I don't know, Tom. But don't you think he looks a little like Jim Madison?"

"I can't see any particular resemblance, Kid—no more than many others bear him. He is rather small and slim—just about Jim's size—black eyes, too; that's about all."

"Perhaps that is all."

Edith then busied herself with feeding a variety of dainties to little Angie, but she cast an occasional furtive glance toward the dark-bearded stranger.

"Don't say any thing, Kid, nor appear to notice him. We will wait and see," said Tom.

Dinner being over, the pleasant afternoon was spent in dancing, swinging and frolicking about the grounds. Every oue there seemed to be happy. Not a drawback of any kind occurred to mar the day's pleasure.

With song and dance and merry frolics the evening also passed, and the pleasure seekers were compelled to relinquish their sports for that day and take to the tents for the night.

As many as could be provided for went with Tom and Edith and spent the night on board their yacht. It was then that a few carelessly asked questions revealed the fact that the dark-bearded stranger was the affianced husband of Belle Winslow.

"But he must be nearly a stranger, is n't he?" asked Tom.

"She met him in San Francisco last Autumn," said

Mary Jones, the daughter of good old Granny Jones. "Belle visited there with her aunt last Winter, you know. He is a Peruvian gentleman and very wealthy—so they say."

"Ah! A Peruvian gentleman, is he?" mused Tom.

"What do you think about Belle's beau, Kid?" asked Tom, when they were alone and ready to retire for the night. "Do you think he is a wealthy Peruvian gentleman?"

"I think he is Jim Madison in disguise," answered Edith. "Do you think so?"

"No, Kid. But we will watch him. If he is Jim he will soon betray his identity."

"Why is it, Tom, that you do not believe he is really Jim?"

"I can not believe that he would dare to come here. He is too big a coward to run such a risk as he would run by coming here," explained Tom.

THE LONG-BEARDED FOREIGNER.

"Is that your only reason, Tom?"

"Yes."

"But if he is partially insane?"

"Well, that would make all the difference in the world. He would be a thousand times more cunning and dangerous under such circumstances than he would otherwise be. But really, Kid, I can hardly think the chap is Jim Madison."

"Perhaps not."

But Edith's suspicions and fears were in no wise allayed by her husband's disbelief that her father's murderer and the bewhiskered Peruvian gentleman were one and the same.

"Well, we will neither worry nor lose sleep over it, Kid." Nor did they.

The second day of the outing was pleasant, and the entire party seemed anxious to get the largest possible measure of enjoyment. So pleasant and agreeable was every one that the day passed almost before they were aware of it, and it was with much regret that the merry sports must be interrupted for another night's rest.

By early dawn, on the third and last day, the picnickers were up and preparing for the return trip, which, like all the other features of the excursion, was a pleasure to the participants.

"After all, it is good to be at home again. Oh, how I love my little home! Tom, I feel that I am getting to be quite a woman now. Don't you think so?"

"Why, yes. I guess that you will pass for a woman, Kid," said Tom. "But why do you think so?"

"Oh, just because I do not care much, any more, for any thing except my home and family. 'My home and family'—don't that sound big, now? Just think of it! How different from a few years back! A poor, homeless and friendless girl then; now a wife and mother! And, oh, so happy!"

Poor Edith! Little did she dream, in her transport of happiness, that ere many days the greatest trouble of her life would come upon her.

A few days after the excursion, Tom Weston, having satisfied himself that the Peruvian gentleman was an assumed character, and having increased suspicion as to the identity of the man, set out for San Francisco. His purpose was to make a thorough investigation of the rich and suave Peruvian gentleman, who had preceded him by a few days to the Sunset City. Should he succeed in identifying him as Jim Madison, his arrest would speedily follow.

"About his trip to San Francisco there is nothing strange or suspicious," said Tom. "But I might as well follow him and settle the question."

So, kissing his wife and baby good-by, he left them in the care of the old house keeper, and set out for the city.

—:o:—

"I Must Call at Granny Jones' and See How She Is."

CHAPTER XLII.

JIM MADISON AND A PAL OVERPOWER EDITH AND TAKE LITTLE ANGIE FROM HER.

It will be remembered that, when Jim Madison made his escape from the asylum, as was reported by the authorities, he had not fully recovered from his insanity.

Now, it appears that in his semi-insane condition, his sole ambition, his very soul itself, seemed wrapped up in the one thought, the one purpose, the one consuming desire—revenge upon Tom Weston for the terrible punishment that he had received at that gentleman's hands.

A mad desire had seized upon his half-crazed mind, long before he made his escape from the asylum, to seek out the home of Tom and Edith Weston and wreak a terrible revenge upon them.

It was with this object in view that he had gone to San Francisco, and it was while there that he had met and become acquainted with the charming Belle Winslow, who was spending the Winter months with her aunt.

Belle was quite a charming girl and had many ardent admirers, but among them all none so much charmed and pleased her as did the dashing, dark-eyed, handsome Peruvian gentleman. Being both rich and handsome, he was considered by many young ladies, and especially by Belle, as a very desirable "catch." He had permitted the impression to get abroad that the object of his visit to the Great Republic of the North was to win for himself an American wife.

It happened that, after his fiery, impetuous fashion—a style that just suited Belle, as she was of a rather wild and impetuous nature herself—he paid court to the damsel and won her heart. He had most ardently pressed his suit, and, when accepted, urged an immediate union. But here the aunt interfered, and, fearing an elopement, had sent the young lady home to her parents, where she arrived a few days before the May Day picnic.

But previous to Belle's return home, Jim Madison—alias Don Alvarez, the wealthy Peruvian—had learned all about Tom and Edith and their surroundings at their new home at Cliffside. He had also learned of Belle's bitter enmity toward little Edith and her almost insane desire to make life miserable for the mistress of Cliffside.

After Belle's return home, as was natural he should do, her betrothed paid her a visit, arriving the day before the picnic. And it was at the picnic dinner that, for the first time since his escape from the asylum and return to America, he saw Tom and Edith.

"Ah, Belle, my love," he said in a whisper, "who is that beautiful girl over there?"

"She is Mrs. Weston."

"And so, she is the charming Edith Weston? And is that little cherub their child?"

"Yes—that is, it is hers, at any rate!"

Poor, deluded Belle! Her Peruvian gentleman was silent, but these were his thoughts:

"Yes, and it is his, too! I know all about that. A curse on you, Tom Weston! Curse you, Edith Beaty! I hate you now as much as—aye, a thousand times more than—I loved you before! I have a plan, and I will execute it. Yes—I will do it, though it cost me my life!"

After his return from the picnic, when he was once more alone, Jim Madison muttered to himself:

"I will send for Bill, the Kidnaper. He is an old friend of mine. He helped me out once, and he will again. He is an old hand at this business, and I must have help. Once I get that kid in my possession, I will bring them to terms. I will wring her heart! Oh, but I will torture you, my little beauty! I will torture you until the suffering you endured before shall seem but a sweet dream, compared with the bitter torment which I will make you feel!"

Once the plan was decided upon, he immediately sent for his friend, the professional kidnaper, who arrived the following day. Soon all their plans were perfected, and they waited only for a favorable opportunity—an opportunity which came all too soon. Tom's trip to San Francisco left the coast clear for the villainous work.

According to their previously arranged plans, the Peruvian gentleman gave notice that he would return to San Francisco. This was the day previous to Tom's departure, and was done to induce him to leave, and also to divert suspicion from Jim. But instead of returning to the city, as was announced that he would, he concealed himself in the neighborhood. He was provided with food and kept posted about the movements of Tom Weston by Belle Winslow, who in her jealous heart, longing for revenge upon her innocent and fortunate rival, as she secretly termed Edith, allowed herself to be used in aiding the villain, even to the extent of becoming an active accessory.

Tom departed for the city, as the plotters expected he would—showing beyond all question of doubt that he had suspected the identity of the bogus Peruvian. Edith and Angie were at home unprotected, and the field was clear for the fiends to accomplish their work. So, now, the part which Belle was to play must be enacted.

Along toward evening, rather late, Belle paid Edith a visit—came to spend the evening with her.

"Tom Departed for the City."

Edith thought nothing strange of this, for Belle often came to see her, in spite of the jealous bitterness which she entertained for her.

"Well," said Belle, ready to return home after an extended and pleasant chat with Edith, "I must call on Granny Jones and see how she is feeling this evening. She was quite sick today, so I heard."

"Granny Jones sick?" cried Edith, anxiously. "Why, I did not know it! Wait a moment, Belle, and I will go over with you."

Edith aroused little Angie from her angel dreams, put on her hood and cloak, and started out with her treacherous companion, thinking only of her dear old neighbor, Granny Jones.

"Let me carry Angie till you are rested," said Belle, as they came to a dark part of the road at the head of the bay, where the great olive trees cast their shadows across the path.

"I thank you, Belle. It is very kind of you."

Little Angie was placed in Belle's outstretched arms.

Almost at the same instant two men rushed from the darkness and wrested the babe from Belle's arms.

Wild with terror, the young mother grappled with the kidnapers, and for a moment it required all the brutal strength of the fiendish Bill to prevent her from regaining possession of the child. But a heavy blow on the temple from the butt of a revolver felled the brave little mother to the ground—bruised and bleeding.

—:o:—

CHAPTER XLIII.

BELLE WINSLOW ELOPES WITH THE PERUVIAN GENTLEMAN —RANSOM FOR ANGIE.

For a moment Belle Winslow stood horrified at the awful work which she had helped to do. What if Edith were dead and the part that she had played were known? In terror she turned from the unconscious girl, who lay stunned and bleeding on the ground, and fled.

Reaching home, Belle gave the alarm, though concealing the identity of the principals. Immediately men set out for the scene of the crime. Here they found Edith, just recovering consciousness.

Heedless of her own hurts—heedless of her torn and blood-stained clothes—the frantic mother, wild with terror, darted away toward home.

On reaching home, she aroused the servants and sent them to the village to give the alarm and start the neighbors in pursuit, while she, running quickly to the stable, mounted her riding pony, without saddle or bridle, and dashed swiftly away toward the nearest telegraph station —some five miles away.

It was no wonder that the operator was dumb with amazement and for a few minutes unable to comply with the frantic mother's request for him to send a message at once to Tom Weston, at the Golden Gate Hotel, San Francisco.

The message read:

'Come quick! They have stolen our baby! EDITH."

"O Granny!" moaned Edith.

Without waiting for an answer, she vanished from the astounded man's presence, and in a moment was flying homeward.

As the frantic mother dashed up to her cottage home and saw the old gardener there, awaiting her return, she cried out to him:

"John! O John! Has any thing been learned?"

"Yes. They've gone north."

But Edith did not wait to hear more. Reining her already foaming horse, she put off along the north road. By daylight she had overtaken the men who were following the trail of the child stealers.

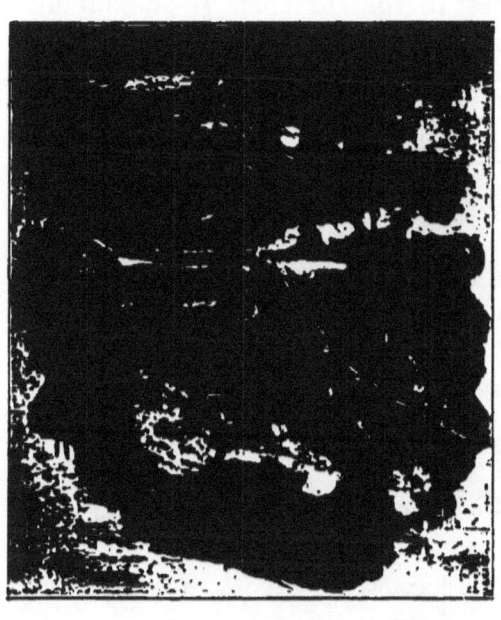

"THE NEAREST TELEGRAPH STATION."

Wild and well nigh breathless, she cried out to them: "Have you learned any thing?"

The men turned away their faces, for they could not bear the sight of the young mother's grief. No one could answer. No one could offer any consolation. Her grief was not of a kind to allow of that, so they all rode on in silence—filled with sympathy they could not express.

Presently they came to a railroad station. Here they learned that two men with a small child had taken the midnight train for San Francisco.

"Telegraph the police!" cried Edith. She gave full description of little Angie, and offered $20,000 for her recovery and the arrest of the kidnapers. Ten minutes later she was on board a train, and soon reached the city.

As she stepped from the train, a man touched her on the arm and said:

"Mrs. Weston, ——"

"What?" cried the girl, so quickly and with such a fierce tone, as she turned her flashing eyes upon him, that for a moment the man was staggered and quite at a loss what to do or say.

"Speak, man! What is it?"

"We have just received a telegram from Mr. Weston, directing us to watch for you here and to inform you that he will come on the noon train," said the man.

"But my baby—what of her? Has any thing been learned of her?"

"Yes, Ma'am. We have traced them to a house near the docks."

"O God!" cried the distracted mother. "Take me there. Why have n't you arrested them? Why have you not rescued my baby? If $20,000 is not reward enough, name your price and deliver my child! Speak, man! Will you take me there?"

"Yes, Mrs. Weston. I will take you there."

He then led the way down into the rogue haunted district of the great city.

A detachment of police had been sent for, and they quickly surrounded the suspected building. An immediate raid was made, and Bill, the Kidnaper, was taken into custody. He, of course, protested his innocence and disclaimed all knowledge of the abduction. Neither Jim nor the babe was found here.

"What shall we do now?" asked the man who had brought Edith there. "We will have a scene. I do hate to tell her."

"Tell her what?" asked Edith, appearing upon the scene. "What is it? Where are they? My baby! Oh, where is my baby?"

As was feared, Edith could bear up no longer, but fell fainting to the floor.

Just as the men were preparing to convey her to a hotel and call a physician, Tom Weston came suddenly upon them.

"Great God! What's this? Speak, man, or by God, I will break every bone in your body!"

"Easy, Tom!"

"Oh, is it you, Mr. Wilson? What is the meaning of this?"

As he asked these questions the loving husband gathered his fainting wife in his arms as though she had been a little child.

"She has fainted, Tom," said Mr. Wilson. "The disappointment at finding her child gone was too much for her."

"How came she wounded?"

"I don't know, Tom. That was done before I met

her. Better take her to a hotel and attend to her first, and then I will come down and see what we can do."

Tom carried her down to the street and entered the carriage which had been summoned. In a few minutes Edith was at the Golden Gate Hotel, in a physician's care.

Restoratives soon brought the poor little mother back to a consciousness of her terrible loss. Brave though she was, this blow was too much for her tender, loving mother-heart, and she gave herself up to inconsolable grief, utterly refusing to be comforted.

"Oh, don't talk of hope and courage! My dear Tom, I can never be happy again!"

"But I will find her, Kid," urged Tom. "I will not let up till I have brought that fiend to account. You shall have your baby again—so help me God, you shall!"

After two weeks of fruitless search, Tom took his broken-hearted wife home to Cliffside, hoping that the sight of the place might revive her. But the effect was the opposite, for every thing about their lovely cottage and its surroundings was intimately associated with little Angie, who had been her inseparable companion during all her residence there.

Weeks passed, and no trace of the child was found. Jim's accomplice—Bill, the Kidnaper—was indicted for a graver crime, previous to this one, and received a sentence of twenty years in the penitentiary.

"No—no!" moaned Edith. "Cliffside can never seem like home to me again."

Many of her neighbors called, but none could offer

any consolation. One look from those despairing eyes was sufficient to convince them that words intended to console would only revive and deepen her grief.

Then came Granny Jones. She sat by the side of the weeping mother for some time in silence. Addressing the husband, she began:

"Mr. Weston, I want to talk with you about this. Have you learned who stole your child?"

"O Granny!" moaned poor Edith, throwing herself on the sofa and weeping bitterly. "Jim Madison and another man took Angie from me."

"We caught one of them, but Jim Madison—if he is the other—got away," said Tom.

"But this Peruvian gentleman—what of him?"

"He is the man!" cried Edith. "He stole my little Angie."

"But he has been here. About two weeks ago he and Belle Winslow went off together—eloped, they call it. Belle told my daughter, Mary, that they were going to Peru."

"Tom," said Edith, arising from the sofa and going up to him, "as sure as there is a God, that man took our baby!"

"And Belle said they were going to Peru, did she?" queried Tom, as he seated Edith in a chair beside him.

"Yes," answered the old lady. "She told Mary not to breathe a word of it to any one, but I made her tell."

"What do you think, Tom?" asked Edith, after Mrs. Jones had gone.

"I will tell you, Kid, just what I think. I think that

Jim intends to keep little Angie till he can arrive at an understanding with us in regard to her restoration. He wants to compel us to let up on him—to let him go free. I think that he will remain near here, for I don't believe that he has any money except what he wins at cards or something of that kind. No matter how much he would like to keep Angie away from us, knowing as he very well does how it tortures you, he dare not keep her long for fear of detection. What he wants is to treat with us, and the sooner he can do it the better it will suit him."

"Can't we hasten the matter by advertising?" asked Edith.

"Yes, Kid. And that is just what we will do. We will send an advertisement tomorrow and have it published, offering to ransom the baby and let the offender go on his own terms."

"But will you do that, Tom?"

"Yes, Kid. *I* will let him go," said Tom, with a strong and suggestive emphasis on the pronoun.

"Ah, I understand," said Edith. "I will see to my part of it. I will nail him to the cross."

Thus it was arranged, and on the morrow the notice was sent to all the country papers and also to some of the leading papers of other cities. After this was done, there was nothing left the bereaved parents but to await the answer.

In the meantime Belle Winslow—Senora Alvarez, as she had thought herself—became aware of her husband's poverty and true character. He required all his ready wit as well as cash to dissuade her from exposing him.

A quick response came to the offer of the anxious parents. Jim made a demand for $10,000 and immunity for "the affair of Angie," as he phrased it, and also for "any previous affair." On these conditions he would, he wrote, "restore the lovely cherub to her rightful owners." Acceptance of his terms would release him from prosecution for four other crimes—the murder of John Beaty, the abduction of Edith, the imprisonment of Weston and complicity in the attempt to destroy Ruby Gulch.

In the course of a week all arrangements were completed, and Tom and Edith set out for San Francisco.

In every preliminary step taken Edith had carefully avoided committing herself to any promise of clemency to Jim Madison—the man who, while protesting ardent love for her, had robbed her of parents and fortune and attempted her utter ruin.

—:o:—

CHAPTER XLIV.

LITTLE ANGIE RESTORED—JIM MADISON DEAD—EDITH'S VOW FULFILLED.

On reaching the city, Tom went at once to the place appointed for the meeting and arranging of the "treaty."

Here he met not only Jim Madison, but his duped consort, Belle. While Tom was arranging for the recovery of little Angie, Edith was arranging with the police to raid the place and capture the criminal.

Without formal greeting, when he was inside the room, Tom began:

"I have come, according to our agreement, for the child. Our agreement has already been made, so there is nothing to talk over. Beside, I have no time to lose, and the sooner this deal is closed the better for all the players."

He handed the money to Belle, with the request that she verify the amount. As Tom did this, he covered Jim with his revolver and commanded:

"Give me the babe."

"You will find the child at this place."

Jim handed Tom a card with street and number written on it, and also some characters which he said would explain matters to the proprietors.

"Yes," said Tom, "but you will go along with me; so lead the way."

With a terrible foreboding in his guilty heart, Jim Madison reluctantly obeyed.

"Here Is the Money."

When the house was reached, Tom was surprised at finding it one of the finest and most respectable looking residences in the fashionable portion of the city. He could hardly believe his senses when he was assured that there was no mistake; that it was the right place.

Their summons was answered by a Negro servant, who ushered them into an elegant parlor, where he left them, after assuring them that the "lady of the house' would soon be there to wait upon them.

Although Tom wondered at the strangeness of the situation, he asked no questions, but waited impatiently for the arrival of the hostess.

Presently the door was opened, and the lady was announced by the black servant as she entered.

Instantly Tom arose, and, handing the card to her, demanded:

"Deliver the child immediately!"

She rang for a servant and instructed her to bring the child. In a few moments she returned with little Angie.

"Here! Give me the child," commanded the woman.

"Curse you—no!" cried Tom, springing before the woman.

"Fool!" cried she. "One word from me, and your life shall pay the forfeit for your rashness!"

"Ha! Ha! Ha!" laughed Jim Madison, and that half-insane look gleamed from his eyes. "Ha! Ha! You are trapped—nicely trapped! Oh, ho!"

Here his gloating was cut short, for a wild-eyed girl dashed through the door, and in an instant seized Angie from the servant's arms and nearly smothered the little creature with her kisses. "My baby! My sweet baby!" cried the little mother, joyously.

But Jim Madison, so suddenly balked in his gloating triumph, failed to see the joyous meeting between little Angie and her mother, for directly behind Edith, as she rushed into the room, he saw with a feeling of impending doom the blue coats of a score of policemen, and he knew that all was up with him.

With a wild look flashing from his snaky eyes, which plainly denoted a sudden fit of insanity, he drew his revolver and fired at Tom. But Tom was on his guard, and, springing aside, the bullet missed him and buried itself in the bosom of Belle Winslow. Before Jim could

"He Drew a Revolver and Fired."

shoot again Tom was upon him, and with a blow from the butt of his revolver knocked the maniac senseless.

"Take him away, and send a physician here quick!" said Tom. Raising the wounded girl, he laid her on a sofa. On Tom's formal complaint, every inmate of the house was placed under arrest, and his $10,000 was returned to him.

Soon a physician came, but a slight examination told him that Belle was mortally wounded.

"She can live but a few hours; there is no hope for her."

"Let us move her to the hotel, where we can see after her," said Tom.

In obedience to this request, the physician had Belle conveyed to the Golden Gate Hotel, where Tom and Edith did all in their power to make the dying girl comfortable and to banish the horror of death which seemed to torment her terribly.

A message was at once sent to the Winslows, with an urgent appeal to start immediately.

Recovering consciousness shortly after her removal to the hotel, Belle confessed the part she had played in the plot, and begged forgiveness.

"Forgive me, Edith! Hear the prayer of a wicked, dying girl! Forgive me, Edith!"

"Yes—I do forgive you," answered Edith. She could not refuse the dying girl's frantic plea. "I forgive you, Belle, and may God forgive you also."

"Oh, how dark it is! How cold—oh, so cold!" She ceased talking, and soon ceased to breathe.

"Poor girl!" sighed Edith. "Pity she could not be spared to see her mother!"

Belle died about midnight—some hours before her parents arrived.

The part which Belle had played as an accomplice of Jim Madison was never known to her parents, and was only told to a trusted few of the neighbors at Cliffside.

Kind-hearted Edith could not bear to wring the mother's heart by letting the awful truth be known.

Jim Madison never recovered from the crushing blow dealt him by the strong arm of Tom Weston. For two months he lingered between life and death, enduring the most intense suffering possible for man, both of body and mind.

For the first three weeks he had been insane—raving and cursing in the most horrible manner. Then his mind cleared, and he became fully cognizant of his deplorable and hopeless condition.

Bad as was his condition in his demented state, it was incomparably worse now, for his guilty and cowardly soul recoiled from death in abject, unutterable fear. At last he sent for Tom and Edith, and with his dying breath he prayed their forgiveness.

"I do not blame you, Tom," he said, feebly.

"Forgive you? Yes. As you are dying, I will forgive you. May God be even more merciful to you!"

Tom then turned his face from that most disgusting of all scenes—a coward writhing in fear.

* * * * * * * * *

What more is there to be told?

Nothing—nothing, save only this:

Tom and Edith, with little Angie, returned to Cliffside in triumph, for their work was done. That irrevocable vow which Edith made over the still, cold form of her dead mother was now fulfilled, and she was free to enjoy the unalloyed happiness which she so deservingly found in the boundless love of one of Nature's noblemen. Added to this good fortune were two possessions—a baby girl and a happy home.

"Thank God!" murmured Edith. "My work is done and I am free!"

—:o:—

TEACHING THE DEAF TO SPEAK.

The Teeth the Best Medium and the Audiphone the Best Instrument for Conveying Sounds to the Deaf, and in Teaching the Partly Deaf and Dumb to Speak.

Address Delivered by R. S. Rhodes, of Chicago, Before the Fourteenth Convention of American Teachers of the Deaf, at Flint, Michigan.

Mr. President and Ladies and Gentlemen:

I would like to relate some of the causes which led to my presence with you to-day.

About sixteen years ago I devised this instrument, the audiphone, which greatly assisted me in hearing, and discovered that many who had not learned to speak were not so deaf as myself. I reasoned that an instrument in the hands of one who had not learned to speak would act the same as when in the hands of one who had learned to speak, and that the mere fact of one not being able to speak would in no wise affect the action of the instrument. To ascertain if or not my simple reasoning was correct, I borrowed a deaf-mute, a boy about twelve years old, and took him to my farm. We arrived there in the evening, and during the evening I experimented to see if he could distinguish some of the vowel sounds. My experiments in this direction were quite satisfactory. Early in the morning I provided him with an audiphone and took him by the hand for a walk about the farm. We soon came across a flock of turkeys. We approached closely, the boy with his audiphone adjusted to his teeth, and when the gobbler spoke in his peculiar voice, the boy was convulsed with laughter, and jumping for joy continued to follow the fowl with his audiphone properly adjusted, and at every remark of the gobbler the boy was delighted. I was myself delighted, and began to think my reasoning was correct.

We next visited the barn. I led him into a stall beside a horse munching his oats, and to my delight he could hear the grinding of the horse's teeth when the audiphone was adjusted, and neither of us could without. In the stable yard was a cow lowing for its calf, which he plainly showed he could hear, and when I led him to the cow-barn where the calf was confined, he could hear it reply to the cow, and by signs showed that he understood their language, and that he knew the one was calling for the other. We then visited the pig-sty where the porkers poked their noses near to us. He could hear them with the audiphone adjusted, and enjoyed their talk, and understood that they wanted more to eat. I gave him some corn to throw over to them, and he signed that that was what they wanted, and that now they were satisfied. He soon, however, broke away from me and pursued the gobbler and manifested more satisfaction in listening to its voice than to mine, and the vowel sounds as compared to it were of slight importance to him, and for the three days he was at my farm that poor turkey gobbler had but little rest.

With these and other experiments I was satisfied that he could hear, and that there were many like him; so I took my grip and audiphones and visited most of the institutions for the deaf in this country. In all institutions I found many who could hear well, and presented the instrument with which this hearing could be improved and brought within the scope of the human voice. But at one institution I was astonished; I found a bright girl with perfect hearing being educated to the sign language. She could repeat words after me parrot-like, but had no knowledge of their value in sentences. I inquired why she was in the institution for the deaf, and by examining the records we learned she was the child of deaf-mute parents, and had been brought up by them in the country, and although her hearing was perfect, she had not heard spoken language enough to acquire it, and I was informed by the superintendent of the institution that she preferred signs to speech. I was astonished that a child with no knowledge of the value of speech should be permitted to elect to be educated by signs instead of speech, and to be so educated in a state institution. This circumstance convinced me more than ever that there was a great work to be done in redeeming the partly deaf children from the slavery of silence, and I was more firmly resolved than ever that I would devote the remainder of my life to this cause.

I have had learned scientists tell me that I could not hear through my teeth. It would take more scientists than ever were born to convince me that I did not hear my sainted mother's and beloved father's dying voice with this instrument, when I could not have heard it without.

THE AUDIPHONE.

It would take more scientists than ever were born to convince me that I did not hear the voice of the Rev. James B. McClure, one who has been dear to me for the last twenty years, and accompanied me on most of my visits to institutions spoken of above, and who has encouraged me in my labors for the deaf all these years, say, as I held his hand on his dying bed only Monday last, and took my final leave from him (and let me say, I know of no cause but this that would have induced me to leave him then), " Go to Flint; do all the good you can. God bless your labors for the deaf! We shall never meet again on earth. Meet me above. Good-by!"

And, Mr. President, when I am laid at rest, it will be with gratitude to you and with greater resignation for the active part you have taken in the interest of these partly deaf children in having a section for aural work admitted to this national convention, for in this act you have contributed to placing this work on a firm foundation, which is sure to result in the greatest good to this class.

You have heard our friend, the inventor of the telephone, say that in his experiments for a device to improve the hearing of the deaf, (as he was not qualified by deafness,) he did not succeed, but invented the telephone instead, which has lined his pocket with gold. From what I know of the gentleman, I believe he would willingly part with all the gold he has received for the use of this wonderful invention, had he succeeded in his efforts in devising an instrument which would have emancipated even twenty per cent. of the deaf in the institutions from the slavery of silence. I have often wished that he might have invented the audiphone and received as much benefit by its use as I, for then he would have used the gold he derives from the telephone in carrying the boon to the deaf; but when I consider that in wishing this I must wish him deaf, and as it would not be right for me to wish him this great affliction, therefore since I am deaf, and I invented the audiphone, I would rather wish that I might have invented the telephone also; in which case I assure the deaf that I would have used my gold as freely in their behalf as would he. [The speaker then explained the use of the audiometer in measuring the degree of hearing one may possess. Then, at his request, a gentleman from the audience, a superintendent of one of our large institutions, took a position about five feet from the speaker, and was asked to speak loud enough for Mr. Rhodes to hear when he did not have the audiphone in use, and by shouting at the top of his voice, Mr. Rhodes was able to hear only two or three "o" sounds, but could not distinguish a word. With the audiphone adjusted to his teeth, still looking away from the speaker, he was able to understand ordinary tones, and repeated sentences after him; and, when looking at him and using his eye and audiphone, the speaker lowering his voice nearly as much as possible and yet articulating, Mr. Rhodes distinctly heard every word and repeated sentences after him, thus showing the value of the audiphone and eye combined, although Mr. Rhodes had never received instructions in lip reading. The gentleman stated that he had tested Mr. Rhodes' hearing with the audiometer when he was at his institution in 1894, and found he possessed seven per cent. in his left ear and nothing in his right.]

FOR THE DEAF.

THE AUDIPHONE

An Instrument that Enables Deaf Persons to Hear Ordinary Conversation Readily through the Medium of the Teeth, and Many of those Born Deaf and Dumb to Hear and Learn to Speak.

INVENTED BY RICHARD S. RHODES, CHICAGO.

Medal Awarded at the World's Columbian Exposition, Chicago,

The Audiphone is a new instrument made of a peculiar composition, posessing the property of gathering the faintest sounds (somewhat similar to a telephone diaphragm), and conveying them to the auditory nerve, through the medium of the teeth. *The external ear has nothing whatever to do in hearing with this wonderful instrument.*

Thousands are in use by those who would not do without them for any consideration. It has enabled doctors and lawyers to resume practice, teachers to resume teaching, mothers to hear the voices of their children, thousands to hear their minister, attend concerts and theatres, and engage in general conversation. Music is heard perfectly with it when without it not a note could be distinguished. It is convenient to carry and to use. Ordinary conversation can be heard with ease. In most cases deafness is not detected.

Full instructions will be sent with each instrument. The Audiphone is patented throughout the civilized world.

: : PRICE : :

Conversational, small size,	$3 00
Conversational, medium size,	3 00
Concert size,	5 00
Trial instruments, good and serviceable,	1 50

The Audiphone will be sent to any address, on receipt of price, by

RHODES & McCLURE PUBLISHING CO.,

Agents for the World,

CHICAGO, ILL.

PUBLISHED BY
RHODES & McCLURE PUBLISHING CO.,
CHICAGO.

All handsomely bound in the best English and American cloths, with full Silver-embossed side and back stamp; uniform in style of binding. Together making a handsome library, or, separately, making handsome center-table volumes.

PRICE, $1.00 EACH. SENT POST-PAID.

ABRAHAM LINCOLN'S STORIES AND SPEECHES; in one volume, complete. New (1897) edition, handsomely illustrated; containing the many witty, pointed and unequaled stories as told by Mr. Lincoln, including Early life stories, Professional life stories, White House and War stories; also presenting the full text of the popular Speeches of Mr. Lincoln on the great questions of the age, including his "First Political Speech," "Rail-Splitting Speech," "Great Debate with Douglas," and his Wonderful Speech at Gettysburg, etc., etc.; and including his two great Inaugurals, with many grand illustrations. An instructive and valuable book; 477 pages.

MOODY'S ANECDOTES; 210 pages, exclusive of engravings. Containing several hundred interesting stories, told by the great evangelist, D. L. Moody, in his wonderful work in Europe and America. Hundreds of thousands of copies have been sold. Illustrated with excellent engravings of Messrs. Moody, Sankey, Whittle and Bliss, and thirty-two full-page engravings from Gustave Dore, making an artistic and handsome volume. "A book of anecdotes which have thrilled hundreds of thousands."—Pittsburg Banner.

MOODY'S GOSPEL SERMONS. As delivered by the great Evangelist, Dwight Lyman Moody, in his revival work in Great Britain and America. Together with a biography of Mr. Moody and his co-laborer, Ira David Sankey. Including, also, a short history of the Great Revival. Each sermon is illustrated with a handsome, full-page engraving from Gustave Dore. The book also contains an engraving of D. L. Moody, Ira D. Sankey, Mr. Moody Preaching in the Royal Opera House, Haymarket, London, Chicago Tabernacle (erected for Mr. Moody's services) and "I Am the Way." A handsome and attractive volume of 443 pages.

MOODY'S LATEST SERMONS. As delivered by the great Evangelist, Dwight Lyman Moody. Handsomely illustrated with twenty-four full-page engravings from Gustave Dore. 335 pages.

MOODY'S CHILD STORIES. As related by Dwight Lyman Moody in his revival work. Handsomely illustrated with sixteen full-page engravings from Gustave Dore and 106 illustrations from J. Stuart Littlejohn. A book adapted to children, but interesting to adults. A handsome volume. Should be in every family. 237 pages.

Standard Publications, $1 each, bound in Cloth.

SAM JONES' GOSPEL SERMONS: 346 pages, exclusive of engravings. Sam Jones is pronounced "one of the most sensational preachers in the world, and yet among the most effective." His sermons are characterized by clearness, point and great common sense, including "hits" that ring like guns. Printed in large type, and illustrated with engravings of Sam Jones and Sam Small, and with nineteen full-page engravings from Gustave Dore.

SAM JONES' LATEST SERMONS. The favor with which Sam Jones' Gospel Sermons has been received by the public has induced us to issue this book of his Latest Sermons. Each sermon is illustrated with a full-page illustration from Gustave Dore's Bible Gallery. The book is bound uniformly with his Gospel Sermons, and contains, besides illustrations, reading matter of 350 pages.

SAM JONES' ANECDOTES; 300 pages. An exceedingly interesting and entertaining volume, containing the many telling and effective stories told by Mr. Jones in his sermons. They strike in all directions and always impart good moral lessons that can not be misunderstood. Adapted for the young and old. A book which everybody can enjoy.

MISTAKES OF INGERSOLL; and his Answers complete; newly revised popular (1897) edition; illustrated, 482 pages. Containing the full replies of Prof. Swing, Judge Black, J. Munro Gibson, D. D., Chaplain McCabe, Bishop Cheney, Dr. Thomas, Dr. Maclauglan, Dr. Goodwin and other eminent scholars to Ingersoll's Lectures on the "Mistakes of Moses,"-"Skulls," "What Shall We Do to be Saved?" and "Thomas Paine," to which are appended in full these Ingersoll lectures and his replies A' fair presentation of the full discussion.

GREAT SPEECHES OF COL. R. G. INGERSOLL; complete; newly revised (1897) edition; 409 pages. Containing the many eloquent, timely, practical speeches of this most gifted orator and statesman, including his recent matchless "Eulogy on Abraham Lincoln," "Speech on the Declaration of Independence," "To the Farmers on Farming," Funeral Oration at his Brother's Grave, etc., etc. Fully and handsomely illustrated.

WIT, WISDOM AND ELOQUENCE OF COL. R. G. INGERSOLL; newly revised popular (1897) edition, illustrated; 336 pages. Containing the remarkable Witticisms, terse, pungent and sarcastic sayings, and eloquent extracts on popular themes, from Ingersoll's Speeches; a very entertaining volume.

THE FIRST MORTGAGE; 310 pages. A truthful, instructive, pleasing and poetical presentation of Biblical stories, history and gospel truth; fully and handsomely illustrated from the world-renowned artist, Gustave Dore, by E. U. Cook, the whole forming an exceedingly interesting and entertaining poetical Bible. One of the handsomest volumes ever issued in Chicago.

Standard Publications, $1 each, bound in Cloth.

 TEN YEARS A COW BOY. A full and vivid description of frontier life, including romance, adventure and all the varied experiences incident to a life on the plains as cow boy, stock owner, rancher, etc., together with articles on cattle and sheep raising, how to make money, description of the plains, etc., etc. Illustrated with 100 full-page engravings, and contains reading matter 471 pages.

WILD LIFE IN THE FAR WEST. By C. H. Simpson, a resident detective, living in this country. Giving a full and graphic account of his thrilling adventures among the Indians and outlaws of Montana—including hunting, hair-breadth escapes, captivity, punishment and difficulties of all kinds met with in this wild and lawless country. Illustrated by 30 full-page engravings, by G. S. Littlejohn, and contains reading matter 264 pages.

A YANKEE'S ADVENTURES IN SOUTH AFRICA. (In the diamond country.) By C. H. Simpson. Giving the varied experiences, adventures, dangers and narrow escapes of a Yankee seeking his fortune in this wild country, which by undaunted courage, perseverance, suffering, fighting and adventures of various sorts is requited at last by the ownership of the largest diamond taken out of the Kimberly mines up to that time, and with the heart and hand of the fairest daughter of a diamond king. Containing 30 full-page illustrations by H. DeLay and reading matter 220 pages.

 WIT. Contains sketches from Mark Twain, witticisms from F. H. Carruth, Douglas Jerrold, M. Quad, Op e Reid, Mrs. Partington, Eli Perkins, O'Malley, Bill Nye, Artemus Ward, Abe Lincoln, Burdette, Daniel Webster, Victor Hugo, Brother Gardner, Clinton Scollard, Tom Hood, L. R. Catlin, Josh. Billings, Chauncey Depew and all humorous writers of modern times. Illustrated with 75 full-page engravings, by H. DeLay, and contains reading matter 407 pages.

BENONI AND SERAPTA. A Story of the Time of the Great Constantine, Founder of the Christian Faith. By Douglas Vernon. A religious novel showing a Parsee's constancy and faith through many persecutions, trials and difficulties, placed in his way by priests, nobles and queens of his time and his final triumph over all obstacles. Being an interesting novel, intended to show the state of the religious feelings and unscrupulous intrigues of those professing religion at the time of the foundation of the Christian faith. Illustrated with 33 full-page engravings, by H. DeLay, and contains reading matter 389 pages.

Standard Publications, $1 each, bound in Cloth.

EVILS OF THE CITIES: By T. DeWitt Talmage, D. D.; 530 pages. The author, in company with the proper detectives, visited many of the most vile and wicked places in New York City and Brooklyn, ostensibly looking for a thief, but in reality taking notes for a series of discourses published in this volume, which contains a full and graphic description of what he saw and the lessons drawn therefrom. The Doctor has also extended his observations to the "Summer Resorts," "Watering Places," Races, etc., etc., all of which are popularized from his standpoint in this volume. Handsomely illustrated and decidedly interesting.

TALMAGE IN THE HOLY LAND: 322 pages. The Palestine Sermons of T. DeWitt Talmage, delivered during his tour of the Holy Land. Including graphic descriptions of Sacred Places, Vivid Delineations of Gospel Truths, interesting local reminiscences, etc., etc., by his visit to the many places made sacred by the personal presence of Jesus and the great pens of Biblical characters and writers. Copiously illustrated.

SIN: A series of popular discourses delivered by T. DeWitt Talmage, D. D., and illustrated with 136 engravings by H. De Lay; 411 pages.

McNEILL'S POPULAR SERMONS: 373 pages. Delivered in London and America by the Rev. John McNeill, one of the ablest and most popular of living divines, and known on both continents as "THE SCOTCH SPURGEON" of Europe, of whom D. L. Moody has said: "He is the greatest preacher in the world." A most clear, vivid, earnest and life-like presentation of Gospel Truth; sincerely and decidedly spiritual. A most edifying, instructive and entertaining volume for young and old.

EDISON AND HIS INVENTIONS: 278 pages. Containing full illustrated explanations of the new and wonderful Phonograph, Telephone, Electric Light, and all his principal inventions, in Edison's own language, generally, including many incidents, anecdotes and interesting particulars connected with the earlier and later life of the world-renowned inventor, together with a full Electrical Dictionary, explaining all of the new electrical terms; making a very entertaining and valuable book of the life and works of Edison. Profusely illustrated.

GEMS OF TRUTH AND BEAUTY. A choice selection of wise, eloquent extracts from Talmage, Beecher, Moody Spurgeon, Guthrie and Parker, forming a volume that keenly interests. A good gift and center table book 300 pages, Illustrated.

WEBSTER'S
Unabridged Dictionary

REPRINT EDITION.

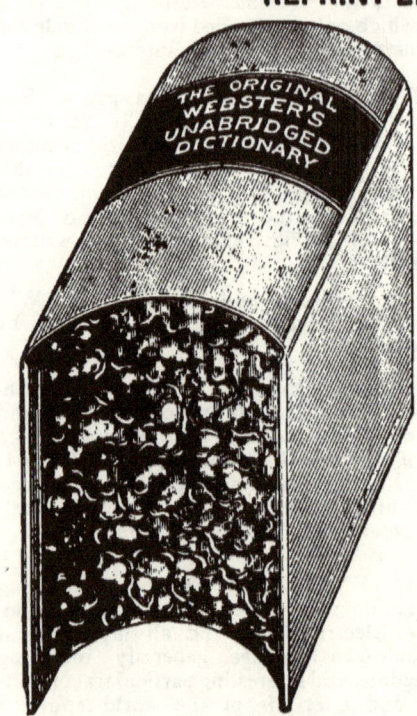

CLOTH, - - - $1.50
HALF MOROCCO, - 1.75
SHEEP, - - - - 2.00

Every School Child Should Have One of These Copies.

OVER 1300 PAGES.

Beautiful Frontispiece of the Flags of All Nations in Five Colors, Illustrated.

THE BEST ON THE MARKET TO-DAY FOR THE MONEY.

ADDRESS ALL ORDERS TO

Rhodes & McClure Publishing Co.,

CHICAGO.

www.ingramcontent.com/pod-product-compliance
Lightning Source LLC
Chambersburg PA
CBHW030308240426
43673CB00040B/1097